*Advance pra*

BC Premier David Eby initially stood by Selina Robinson when the Jewish NDP MLA and cabinet minister made an ill-advised comment about the land on which the State of Israel was founded.

But when NDP members, donors and the Muslim community called for Robinson's ouster, Eby showed her the door, then tried to portray her departure as a mutual decision.

Consigned to the backbench, Robinson proposed to conduct an outreach to the Jewish and Muslim communities. The Premier's Office rejected the offer, prompting her to quit the NDP caucus.

Robinson's rough treatment by Eby is the focus of a book where she details her struggle against antisemitism in the NDP.

"I did not leave my Premier and my party," she writes persuasively. "They left me."

**Vaughn Palmer**
Provincial political columnist, *Vancouver Sun*

* * *

Selina shines such a vital light on how deeply troubling and pervasive the ongoing antisemitism is towards the Jewish community in BC and Canada, and how the lack of voice and silence around the fight against antisemitism undermines civil society for all of us. Her story is truly a testament to the integrity and the courage to act that we need from our leaders, and from each other.

**Michael Lee**
Former BC Liberal / BC United MLA

* * *

It was an otherwise inoffensive and offhand remark in a passing reference to an historical fact relating to the birth of the State of Israel. That's all. But it was sufficient to serve as the pretext for the public lynching of a Jewish cabinet minister by a nominally progressive provincial government, in Canada, in 2024.

Selina Robinson was that cabinet minister, and this is her story. It's a candid and vivid account of the humiliation she was forced to endure, but it's much more than that. It's a testament that bears witness to the depravity that engulfed Canada during the weeks and months following the Simchat Torah pogrom of October 7, 2023, when paroxysms of antisemitic violence and hysteria burst to the surface across the country.

It is no small thing that among the organizations celebrating Robinson's persecution was the Popular Front for the Liberation of Palestine, in Ramallah. In a statement from the notorious terrorist organization's Central Media Office, the PFLP had this to say: "The downfall of a minister biased towards the Zionist entity in Canada is an important precedent."

And it was an important precedent. Selina Robinson's political career wasn't destroyed for anything she'd said. It was because of who she is. A Zionist, and a Jew.

**Terry Glavin**
Author and journalist

* * *

Selina Robinson's memoir unveils the intense political and personal fallout from a single, ill-chosen phrase. With honesty and resilience, Robinson explores antisemitism, public service, and the unexpected challenges of her career. Her journey through criticism, cancer, and courage offers a powerful reflection on integrity and justice in leadership.

As a Jewish cabinet minister, Robinson faced harsh public attacks. But it was the failure of her NDP colleagues to stand by her that ultimately led to her departure from politics. Despite conversations with Premier David Eby about the antisemitism she encountered, her concerns were ignored, leaving her isolated.

This memoir exposes the dangers of political silence, the cost of standing alone, and the profound impact of moral leadership—or its absence—on democracy and personal integrity. Robinson's story resonates as a poignant exploration of courage, accountability, and the urgent need for principled leadership.

**Jas Johal**
CKNW host, and former Global National Asia
Bureau Chief and former BC Liberal MLA

Jewel,
all the best
Selina

# TRUTH BE TOLD

# TRUTH BE TOLD

Selina Robinson

*Truth Be Told*


selinarobinsonbook@gmail.com

ISBN 978-1-0691651-0-7 (paperback)
ISBN 978-1-0691651-1-4 (eBook)

Cover art: Kathleen Tennant

For John Horgan
(1959–2024)

A friend, a leader and a mensch who understood and lived *tikkun olam*—making the world a better place.

# *Contents*

# *Acronyms*

BC NDP—British Columbia New Democratic Party

BDS—Boycott, Divestment and Sanctions

BLM—Black Lives Matter

CT—computerized tomography

CTA—Coquitlam Teachers Association

CUPE—Canadian Union of Public Employees

GPA—grade point average

IDF—Israel Defence Forces

IHRA—International Holocaust Remembrance Alliance

IJV—Independent Jewish Voices

MLA—Member of the Legislative Assembly

MP—Member of Parliament

NIMBY—Not in My Back Yard

SD 47—School District 47

UBC—University of British Columbia

# *Preface*

THIS BOOK IS NOT about the history of Jews, or Palestinians, or an analysis of Middle East politics. There are others who have written volumes on these topics. This book is also not about what specific actions the world needs to take to help bring peace to the region. There are others whose careers and experiences make them more qualified than me for that discussion.

This book is about the choices that Canadians and our leaders can make to either support peace or create greater division both here in Canada and in the Middle East. Calling for the death or destruction of the other is not a path to peace. Vilifying or dehumanizing the other is not a path to peace. Yet too many Canadians and others around the world have chosen this path.

The way to peace is to support dialogue, to encourage relationships, to discover common humanity and to work together to forge a shared path to harmony both in Canada and around the world. Too many Canadians and others right now are not doing this. Their voices say peace but their actions advance intolerance, intransigence and violence.

I am a progressive Jew and a Zionist who believes in a two-state solution through which both the Palestinian and the Israeli peoples find self-determination, peace and fulfilment.

I disagree with the current Israeli government's policies and practices on many issues, including many of their actions in Gaza and the West Bank.

I also disagree with the Palestinian leaders in the West Bank and the terrorist regimes in the Gaza Strip and elsewhere who seek to destroy Israel at the cost of the well-being of more Palestinian generations.

Palestinians and Israelis both have the right to a homeland, to security and to live without fear. Both peoples need leaders with a vision for coexistence and peace.

This is what I want for Palestinians and Israelis.

What I want for Canadians is for us to advance that ideal, rather than obstruct it. Every time we advance an intolerant position that we view as "pro-Israel" *or* "pro-Palestinian," I want us to understand that it is neither. We need to be both. To be "pro-Palestinian," we must also be "pro-Israel" and vice-versa. This is the only way to advance peace in the Middle East, for both sides to win some and both sides to lose some. That is the essence of compromise. No single people can prevail "from the river to the sea." We must strive for peace from the river to the sea. That means coexistence and two states. It is possible. If we abandon that hope, we abandon all hope.

For Canadian Jews, peace will only come when Canadians address antisemitism here in our country. We must recognize antisemitism as a *Canadian* problem and not pretend it is a product of foreign events. Most overseas conflicts do not cause this level of racism and violence against minority communities in this country—why does this one? It is because of a pre-existing strain in our society. All Canadians need to acknowledge and confront that the way we do other forms of racism and intolerance.

This book is about that problem—and how Canadians must stand up and address it.

This is a book that shares the experiences of one Jewish Canadian politician—but I share my story for this larger purpose: to shine a little light on how antisemitism manifests in

Canada and how our leaders are failing to confront it. Leaders—and I use this term broadly because another tenet of this book is that each of us has it within us to be a leader—are not successfully advancing peace in the world or multicultural harmony at home. Too often, we are dividing our own society and rewarding continued intolerance and war abroad.

In these pages, I try to show how we can reverse this tendency, how we can all practice *tikkun olam*, the Jewish value of repairing the world or, as I understand it, the obligation to make the world a better place for everyone. By sharing in this story, you are taking a step toward a better world.

# *Four Fateful Words*

*Crappy piece of land.*

THESE ARE THE FOUR Fateful Words that ended my career. Or at least that is how the story goes.

In reality, these words were used to take down a British Columbia cabinet minister who some people had been targeting for months.

It was sloppy language, nothing more, but it provided the *Gotcha!* for anti-Israel extremists to build a case that I was racist, Islamophobic, intolerant and an evil monster that needed to be cancelled.

In an ideal world, it would have been the extremists who were dismissed, not me. In an ideal world, we would be blessed with leaders who can differentiate between right and wrong.

Leadership means making tough choices, standing against intimidation and threats, and holding firm when confronted with unjust attacks. In an ideal world, this is what would have happened in the aftermath of my remarks.

On January 30, 2024, I participated in an online panel of four Jewish Canadian officials—a Member of Parliament, an Ontario cabinet minister, a Senator, and me—who came together to share our reflections on the massive spike in antisemitism in the aftermath of the atrocities perpetrated against Israelis and other victims on October 7, 2023.

As British Columbia's Minister of Post-Secondary Education and Future Skills, I had particular insights into the situation on campuses, where the atmosphere for Jewish students was unprecedentedly challenging.

By the time my turn came to speak, the webinar was behind schedule. I was racing, somewhat, to make my points. I do not say this as an excuse but merely as an explanation. I remember feeling that my mouth was getting ahead of my brain. I was searching for words to condense the points I wanted to make. After more than a dozen years as an elected official, I have honed my speaking skills and I know now—I think I knew in the moment, on the webinar—that I was getting sloppy.

Here is the point I was trying to make: Young Canadians do not know the history of Jewish people. Surveys indicate that vast numbers of young people know little to nothing about antisemitism or the Holocaust and even less about the creation and history of the modern State of Israel. Without this foundational knowledge of the Holocaust or of centuries of antisemitism, how Jewish people have been scapegoated again and again across societies and centuries of Jewish statelessness, young Canadians cannot appreciate the contemporary Jewish experience. Without any awareness of the challenges overcome by Israelis, or about the astonishingly successful society they have built in the face of incessant threats and attacks, young people cannot develop reasoned opinions about what is happening now.

I wanted people to understand that, despite all the overblown anti-Israel rhetoric, Israelis have tried tirelessly to live in coexistence with their neighbours—while providing a near-miraculous model of postwar decolonization and an example of successful statecraft on a foundation of little more than rock and dust.

"We have a whole generation," I said in the webinar, "and we know from the data that it is 18-to-34-year-olds, that have no idea about the Holocaust. They don't even think it happened.

They don't even understand that Israel was offered to the Jews who were misplaced, displaced, so they have no connection to how it started. They don't understand that it was a crappy piece of land with nothing on it. It couldn't grow things, it didn't have anything on it."

I caught myself. I corrected.

"There were several hundred thousand people, but other than that, it didn't produce an economy," I said.

I did not mean to dismiss the human beings who lived there. I was making the point that this was land with little inherent agricultural value and that there was effectively no industry or economic development there. That is not a slight against the people living there. If anything, it is a statement about Ottoman and British imperialism and their neglect of the land's people.

Something else I said in the webinar also attracted criticism—and rightly so. I made an allusion to First Nations that I very much regret. I was trying to make a point about the disproportionate engagement activists have with Israel and Palestine, something I believe is verging on obsession and that has a lot to do with the fact that the conflict involves Jews. I made a clumsy comparison with First Nations here at home.

I had been told by an Indigenous leader several years ago that if there is conflict between two First Nations, it is up to those nations to sort through their conflict—other nations don't interfere unless invited. I attempted to echo that sentiment and said, "If there was a conflict between the Tsleil-Waututh and the Squamish Nations over a piece of land, would we weigh in, regular people?" I said.

I am mortified that I used "regular people" when I meant "nonindigenous people." I don't even remember the word "regular" coming through my head and out my mouth. Was that internalized anti-Indigenous racism? I remember feeling at a loss for words and rushing my remarks. For that, I absolutely apologize.

Interestingly, this was not the misstatement that got me fired. The words they "got" me on—"crappy piece of land"—were relatively harmless.

If I had not spoken those words, though, would I have remained in cabinet? That is by no means certain.

If I hadn't been sloppy in my language on that day, those who were out to get me probably would have found something I said a day later, a week later, or a month later. They were determined to find something.

Again, in an ideal world, even this poor choice of words would have quickly blown over. In a context that was not already overwrought with rage and absent a cadre of activists determined to see me brought down, my apology would have been a one-day story, if that.

Instead, "crappy piece of land" became blood in the water.

* * *

What happened to me in the next week is, in the grand scheme, immaterial. What happens to a single individual is of primary importance mostly to that person and those who care about them. Politicians come and go. Some make a positive impact, others are forgotten. Whatever history does or does not remember of me, I will be content with.

My reason for sharing this story is less about me than it is about the transcendent values that are threatened by what happened. The lessons that my individual story impart are about how leaders respond to political conflicts, how they balance principles with expediency. Above all, my story contains lessons for anyone who believes in multiculturalism, antiracism and, above all, democracy.

This is a story about antisemitism and how it ended the career of one Jewish official. But it is more than that. It is about the necessity of good people—especially people elected to positions of leadership—to stand up when an individual or group is targeted. It is also a lesson about the dangers of silence, of caving to coercion, of going along to get along.

This book is about what *happened*. More importantly, it is a story about what that *means*. Above all, this book is a cautionary tale, a warning. I also hope it is an uplifting and inspirational reference for people who truly want to advance progress, peace, coexistence and human understanding. At the end, I advance some tangible steps people can take to engage in what Jews call *tikkun olam*—making the world a better place.

For people outside British Columbia or Canada, I hope this story will be interesting and relatable. I have attempted to extrapolate truly universal and urgent lessons about the capacity of a single individual to make positive change in the world. Just by reading this book, you are engaging in tikkun olam, because all profits from sales of this book will go to advance coexistence between Israelis and Palestinians and fight antisemitism in Canada.

Throughout the process of writing this book, the words of British Columbia's Premier David Eby have echoed in my mind. In the aftermath of my "crappy piece of land" remark, and after I was fired, the Premier publicly announced that the reason I needed to step away from my file was because of "the depth of work" that I needed to do to repair the damage I had caused.

This book is that deep work.

## *Everything Changes*

ON OCTOBER 6, 2023, I was overjoyed to receive the news that the cancer I had been fighting had disappeared. I had been living with cancer—let me rephrase that: *cancer had been living with me*—since 2006. I had kept it at bay with daily oral chemotherapy but, after 15 years of treatment, my oncologist thought we had completely eradicated it. I stopped taking my pills, but my cancer returned in February of 2023. After returning to my familiar regimen of chemotherapy, my oncologist gave me the best news I could have hoped for—the tumour had disappeared, the chemotherapy was back doing its job.

We had so much to celebrate. My husband Dan and I enjoyed a special dinner at a Thai restaurant not far from our home in Coquitlam, our suburb east of Vancouver.

When we arrived home, it was late and I was tired. But I turned on the TV before heading to bed.

Late evening Vancouver time is early morning in the Middle East—there, it was October 7, 2023. The banners blared across the bottom of the screen that Israel was under attack.

I went online, cable news still blasting images at me, my panic increasing. I assimilated instantly that what had happened was different from the incessant terror attacks Israelis had experienced over their country's 75 years of existence.

As the scenes of horror flashed, I thought of the Israelis closest to me. My daughter, Leya, and her partner, Omer, are Israelis.

Leya, who moved to Israel five years before and became a citizen, had returned to the Vancouver area several months earlier. Omer had arrived in Canada as a permanent resident just a week before, on September 30. He was beginning a new life in Canada, embraced by our family.

This horrific act of terrorism, the magnitude of which I was only beginning to grasp, would be devastating for him, as it would be for all Israelis. I worried that he would want to go back to Israel, to join his Israel Defence Forces unit if they were called up to serve in what was likely to become another full-on war.

While I knew this moment would be life-altering for all Israelis, I knew it would also be a turning point for Jews around the world. This was not something that required thinking. It was intuitive. What happens *over there*, affects Jews *over here*. Conflict *there* always results in conflict *here*.

While my mind was on the victims in Israel, my gut knew the repercussions would reach very close to home.

Every Jew everywhere would be affected. I also understood instinctively that these events would have specific impacts for Jews who live our lives in progressive circles.

Jews like me.

I was the most prominent Jewish voice in British Columbia's government—I had proudly dubbed myself the "Jew in the Crew" and that light-hearted moniker would take on far more serious meaning now. All of these realizations descended on me amid the chaos I was seeing online and on TV. I knew that I would have to step up for my community. I also knew that my government would need me to help steward them through the Jewish community's grief and trauma. More than ever, I would need to interpret the government for my community and interpret my community for the government.

And I knew that my world—my personal world, my professional world, the way I see the world and the way the world sees me—would be different.

* * *

In the following days, we would slowly comprehend the depth and breadth of what had happened. The numbers, repellent as they are, cannot capture what we are still assimilating as the inhumane brutality that occurred that day. It was the intent of the perpetrators to inflict not just death, but maximal emotional and physical trauma as well.

Because of the chaos of the day, numbers remain uncertain. Early reports said more than 3,000 terrorists, some of them in a state of extreme agitation from the amphetamine Captagon, invaded Israel at 30 different breached locations, including from the sky using powered paragliders. More recent numbers from the Israel Defence Forces suggest twice that number of Palestinians crossed into Israel that day, including 3,800 trained and armed Hamas terrorists and waves of other Palestinians who entered Israel to join in the violence and loot the valuables of the murdered and fleeing Jews.

In all, they murdered 1,139 people, including 364 young people at a music festival, 36 children, dozens of foreign nationals, and numerous Arab citizens of Israel. The terrorists took 251 people, including a nine-month-old baby and 41 other children, as well as the bodies of some victims already murdered, as hostages into the Gaza Strip. Sexual violence was rampant, with rape and sexual mutilation of women and men. The terrorists used toxic gases that suffocated victims. Entire families were murdered as parents shielded their children. People were burned alive. The testimony of survivors is beyond endurance.

Hours of video footage is in the public realm, documentation by the perpetrators of what they considered their proudest moments.

These are the acts celebrated by some people worldwide as heroic "resistance."

History has stolen much of our capacity to be surprised by innovations in barbarism, but to understand October 7 and the enemy that Israel is facing demands our exposure to these realities. Human events are quantitative—we can count the dead and wounded—but they are also qualitative, and the atrocities perpetrated that day speak to a level of inhumanity that demands our attention. We must not only mourn these victims but address how a society could produce perpetrators of acts like these.

It is crucial for the world to understand that Hamas is not, primarily, a movement for the liberation of Palestine. It is an explicitly antisemitic, fundamentalist, Islamist movement whose 1988 charter states: "Israel will exist and will continue to exist until Islam will obliterate it, just as it obliterated others before it." This is not a movement for the national liberation of Palestine. It is a movement for the annihilation of Israel.

Israel has faced war and terrorism before. Since before Israel's inception as an independent state, the Jewish people of that region have been under systematic attack. Periodically, these threats break into open warfare. More routinely—if death and destruction can ever be routine—Israelis have faced terrorism in the form of stabbings, shootings, bombs on buses and in discotheques, missiles falling from the sky and a panorama of crimes that have taken thousands of lives and left exponentially more people with lifelong injuries.

October 7, 2023, was different.

We knew instantly that October 7 was singular not only in scope, but in kind. October 7 was unique because it struck not only Israel's physical safety, but the emotional security of Israelis and of Jews worldwide.

Israel was created, among other reasons, to ensure that the Jewish people would never again be indefensible in a scenario where people sought to murder entire families in their homes, to torture, terrorize, rape, murder and perpetrate genocide against us without coordinated resistance.

Many people lack knowledge of Jewish history and so do not appreciate the centrality of Israel to Jewish people everywhere. This was the problem I was trying to articulate when I was hoisted on my petard of crappy land. The connection Jews have to Israel is deeply ingrained. The connection is personal, spiritual, familial and historical.

The failure to appreciate this connection results in a disordered understanding of overseas events and how those events affect Jewish Canadians.

Jewish and many non-Jewish Canadians have been living in different realms since October 7. What many people perceive as political discourse—at worst as "anti-Zionism"—most Jewish people hear, to varying degrees, as nonchalance about the value of Jewish lives.

This is a fundamental rupture in the dialogue. It is something that non-Jewish people must understand if they want to comprehend their Jewish neighbours' reactions to October 7 and everything that has happened since.

October 7 went to our very essence. It evoked a time before Jewish self-determination, when Jewish homes were invaded with impunity, our right to life abrogated, our inherent dignity spat upon in the most inhumane ways. It reminded us of earlier times when individuals and families were ripped from their homes and dragged into a place of dystopic and unrelenting cruelty and annihilation.

For any people, an attack like October 7 would have been an unimaginable atrocity. For Jewish people, whether Israelis or not, these acts of rape, torture, immolation, kidnapping and mass murder were an attack on our most intrinsic fears and deep historical memories. For some of us, they triggered intergenerational trauma.

The existence of Israel has never been a guarantee that Jewish people will not be attacked or murdered—the past 75 years have proven that beyond a doubt. But the existence of Israel means, at least, that Jewish people will never again be without a collective defence against such attacks. The failures of the Israeli government and military to prevent October 7 will be subject to assessment for years to come. But the impact of that failure plagues almost every Jew with personal or historical memories of a time when we were entirely at the whim of violent neighbours who might rise up at any moment and take Jewish lives in the most brutal ways.

Jewish people have experience, within the memory of the oldest generation still living, of despotic leaders issuing explicit, brazen promises to eradicate the Jewish people from the face of the earth. These elders speak of how the world stood by, abandoning the Jews of Europe to their fate.

The Holocaust was not an aberration, but part of a long trajectory of antisemitism. It was unique in its devastating impacts because of the geographic reach of the Nazis and the assembly line method of mass killing they employed. But it was part of a much longer history—and that history did not end in 1945.

It is also important to understand that the Holocaust happened not only because of the Nazis and their collaborators. Its magnitude was possible only because the entire world abandoned the Jewish people in our moment of greatest need.

At the Évian Conference, in 1938, 32 Western countries gathered to discuss the plight of Europe's Jews in the face of Hitler's expressed goal of annihilation.

The response was almost unanimous. The world would leave the Jews to Hitler's devices. The Dominican Republic, alone among the countries of the world, agreed to accept some Jewish refugees—but by then it was too late. The Jewish people's window for escape had slammed shut.

Four months after those countries convened at Évian-les-Bains and sent a collective message to Hitler that he was free to do to the Jews as he chose, the Nazis perpetrated Kristallnacht. This was an organized, top-down pogrom of murderous, destructive Jew-hatred intended to look like a spontaneous, populist uprising. This is widely seen as the moment the rhetorical and legislative antisemitism of the Nazi regime veered into uninhibited violence, the real beginning of the Holocaust. Kristallnacht was a directive from the Nazis. But it was a result of the green light the free world, convened at Évian, gave Hitler.

Had there been a single state where Jewish people controlled the immigration policy—indeed, had Western countries including Canada demonstrated any concern about whether Jews lived or died—six million lives might have been saved. Canada's own record at this time is shameful. Pondering how many endangered Jewish refugees our country should accept, our top immigration official declared, "None is too many."

For Jews, in addition to all the other personal, familial, spiritual and other connections, this is one of the crucial reasons Israel matters.

Jewish statelessness, a history almost unknown to non-Jews, or at least rarely considered by them, is a lesson most Jewish people have learned. This is just one reason why Israel holds a special place for Jews worldwide, even those who have never set foot there. Israel is, among many things, an insurance policy, a safe room, a refuge of last resort. It is the world's only Jewish state.

This is not, as is sometimes said, an example of a unique Jewish "persecution complex" or a "victim mentality." This is an entirely appropriate response to history and current events.

Since long before October 7, Jews have watched and listened as today's despotic leaders have promised to annihilate the Jewish people. Hamas has a long history of broadcasting their genocidal intentions. The Iranian regime, which provides monetary and material support to Hamas, Hezbollah and other terrorists groups, has repeatedly promised to wipe Israel from the map and they are developing nuclear weapons to do just that.

Far too often, these realities are met with indifference. The world acts as though Jews are overreacting. They say we are hypersensitive. They insist that the blood-soaked rhetoric of Israel's enemies—enemies who do not make the polite distinction between "Zionists" and "Jews"—is little more than bluster some Arab and Iranian leaders use for domestic audiences. The ayatollahs, they argue, wouldn't dare nuke Israel because it would be mutually assured destruction.

To the Jewish people, the world says: *Relax, what's the worst that could happen?*

This is the context in which most Jewish Canadians perceived October 7. What happened next, though, has shaken almost every Jew to our core.

We were used to the casualness with which the world responds to threats and attacks against Israel. We have become too familiar with the cacophony of condemnation every time Israel defends itself. We are familiar with the regular accusations and double standards applied to Israel from activists, commentators, nongovernmental organizations and the United Nations. Libels that range from apartheid to genocide and every denunciation in between.

What we had not seen before was the multi-front phenomenon that came next. People worldwide *celebrated* October 7. They gathered at rallies in Vancouver and around the world and jubilantly celebrated the mass murders, rapes, beheadings, immolations, kidnappings and other atrocities. This was new.

As the war Hamas started heartbreakingly progressed, and as images of Palestinian deaths spread across our screens, Jewish people worldwide were increasingly targeted with hateful messages by our neighbours.

We witnessed shootings at Jewish schools and fire-bombings of synagogues. Jewish businesses were defaced and their owners threatened. Bomb threats were issued against Jewish institutions, including preschools, creating a constant sense of underlying peril. CBC reported that, at an anti-Israel rally in Montréal three weeks after October 7, Adil Charkaoui, an imam, publicly prayed, "Allah, take care of these Zionist aggressors. . . . identify them all, then exterminate them. And don't spare any of them." At other rallies, activists have chanted "Long live October 7!" Jewish school kids have been told by classmates to "go back to the gas chambers."

Less dangerous but far more prevalent has been the constant drip of what might be called microaggressions, signs everywhere that people like us are not welcome: Hateful messages on telephone poles in our neighbourhoods, community Facebook groups that have nothing to do with the Middle East erupting into vitriol that feels very personal to us. Stickers on Israeli products in grocery stores declaring "This product supports genocide."

Incidents like these are happening in Canada on a daily basis.

Jews have responded with differing levels of anxiety. Some are removing their mezuzahs, the small case with sacred verses that Jews place on our doorframes. Others are putting baseball caps over their kippas and hiding their Jewish star necklaces.

Some parents are telling their kids to keep quiet about anything that could identify them as Jews. Some are even moving to neighbourhoods where there are more Jews so they feel safer among their neighbours—or leaving Canada entirely for Israel.

Police and governments struggle to maintain statistics on the astronomical rise in antisemitic incidents. And when we express our concerns about all of this, we often face a shocking dismissal.

A core trope of antisemitism, one that allows many people to ignore the problem, is that Jews have a "persecution complex," that we are needlessly hypersensitive, that we "cry wolf."

These ideas—themselves a form of antisemitism—may allow even good people, antiracist people, to dismiss our concerns. It is a circular, self-fulfilling form of anti-Jewish racism: The more we warn that the atmosphere is dangerous, the more some people accuse us of exaggerating.

There is something else happening, though. There is a callous response that we see often on social media. It is a vicious bit of dismissiveness that has no place in a multicultural society.

Expressed Jewish concerns about antisemitism often elicit something like: *Now you know how Palestinians feel* or *Palestinians are dying and you are complaining about microaggressions?*

This is something we see in almost no other context: Canadians reacting to one group's expressions of concern around racism with the retort, *What about this other group's concerns?*

Pain is not a zero-sum game. Two things can be true at once. A horrific war with far too many dead can be happening in the Middle East and antisemitism in Canada can be alarming and demand addressing.

Amid all this, we have seen something that is perhaps the most concerning of all.

While small clusters of truly depraved individuals are celebrating October 7, and large numbers of well-intentioned but misguided activists rage against Israel rather than rallying for peace and coexistence, Jewish Canadians have watched the vast majority of Canadians, including many we thought were our friends, remain silent as we share our expressions of isolation, fear and abandonment.

In a time of deep sadness and hurt, this silence has often been the greatest hurt of all.

So many Jews have had flashbacks to the lessons of our grandparents—stories of bystanders and collaborators, of neighbours pointing out where Jews live, stories my generation of Jews had dismissed as a thing of the past.

But there are also stories of upstanders, of righteous individuals and groups who came to the rescue in the bleakest moments, and at lethal risk to themselves and their families.

The risks to righteous people in most countries right now are not like they were in those earlier times—and, of course, the situation Jews face in Canada does not come anywhere near to the histories our grandparents warned us about. But this is precisely why the lack of vigilance is so concerning. The dangers of speaking up are minimal. Yet still the silence remains. This has caused many Jewish people, including me, to ask ourselves: *Who would hide me?*

When people like me and my children see neighbours celebrating the mass murder of Jews, we expect righteous people to stand up and stand by us. We have been raised with the knowledge of what can happen when good people choose to do nothing.

We know from public opinion polls that Canadians recognize that antisemitism has reached dangerous levels. Most Canadians are empathetic to Jewish people—and they recognize that Israel needs to defend itself. This is what they overwhelmingly tell opinion pollsters.

Yet, too often, they remain silent.

What I saw, at the highest levels of one Canadian provincial government, was not righteous behaviour. It was, in several instances, what I experienced as overt antisemitism. In far more cases, it was indifference in the face of these incidents. It was, when it mattered most, ostensible leaders who appeared to put politics and expediency ahead of principles and moral clarity.

Above all, I experienced silence where I should have experienced allyship.

If this could happen to a senior elected official in the government of a progressive political party committed to antiracism and inclusion, this is a symptom of something serious.

It is past time for Canadians to have a frank discussion about antisemitism. Like the conversations we have undertaken in recent years around race, gender, Indigenous reconciliation, privilege and other tough issues, it is time we had that hard talk about antisemitism.

As much as this book is about my story, my experience serves merely as a case study and an opening to engage in a very much overdue dialogue about Jews and anti-Jewish racism.

Let us begin that conversation.

# *It Hits the Fan*

ON JANUARY 30, 2024, a Tuesday night, I spoke on the B'nai Brith Canada panel where I uttered the Four Fateful Words. By Thursday, the Twitterverse was all lit up.

If there were any remaining doubts that there was a mob out to get me, this cleared matters up. Consider: A webinar with four talking heads convened by a right-leaning Canadian Jewish advocacy organization is not exactly prime time TV. The fact that it took mere hours for my words to flash across social media and leap over to dominate the news cycle by early Thursday indicates that some people were very interested in what I had to say—and not because they were fans.

Within hours, things were wild. I was being accused of Islamophobia, supporting genocide and all sorts of other crimes and misdemeanours. This social media witch hunt seemed coordinated—even the terrorist organization the Popular Front for the Liberation of Palestine chimed in. My community office inbox was flooded with emails calling for my resignation.

I was working with the Premier's Office to respond, and I let Premier David Eby know directly that his communications team and I were on it. On Thursday at 3 PM, I sent the Premier a text: "Sorry. I got lazy . . . Should have been more precise with my words. Apology crafted. Should be out soon."

At 3:10 PM, he responded: "Happens to the best. Hang in there."

Twenty minutes later, I let him know that I had also reached out to the National Council of Canadian Muslims to apologize. I was doing what I could to address the perceived wrong.

I was assured that the Premier had my back, and I was clear that I would fully apologize for any offence. The Premier's Office drafted the apology for me, I reviewed it and signed off on it for release.

"I want to apologize for my disrespectful comment referring to the origins of Israel on a 'crappy piece of land.' I was referring to the fact that the land has limited natural resources," I said. "I understand that this flippant comment has caused pain and that it diminishes the connection Palestinians also have to the land. I regret what I said and I apologize without reservation."

That apology did nothing to calm the outrage. We tried a second apology on Friday, but that didn't have any more impact than the first one. Social media continued to be aflame with calls for my firing—and worse.

On Friday, I attended a Tri-Cities Chamber of Commerce event hosting the four area MLAs. I had the fortune of sitting with the Kwikwetlam First Nation leadership and I was chatting with one of the elected council members, a lovely, kind man. He reminded me that the people yelling at me don't know me and that those who know me know what's in my heart, that there is no malice there. He suggested that I take a walk down to the river and cast a few stones into the water to take away the hurt and the pain that was starting to build in my heart.

Not only were his words what I desperately needed to hear at that moment, but there was a magnificent cross-cultural symmetry. In Jewish tradition, on Rosh Hashanah, the new year, we perform Tashlich. We symbolically cast our sins into flowing water, traditionally in the form of breadcrumbs, and in more recent times, stones (because bread is not good for birds). I am still so appreciative of his words because they helped get me through what would become some of the most difficult hours I have ever endured.

Sleep was elusive that night and into the weekend. The idea of eating made me nauseous. I could not focus on anything, so I took out a 1,000-piece jigsaw puzzle and laid it out on the dining room table for something to focus on that didn't require anything more than the little energy I had.

Some members of the legislative Press Gallery had reached out to me that Friday to see how I was holding up. They advised me to hold steady, that the noise should subside by the end of the weekend.

Perhaps they had not seen, at that point, the message from more than a dozen imams, mosques and Islamic centres, accusing me of "blatant bigotry" and telling the Premier that, unless I was fired, New Democrat MLAs and candidates would not be permitted in their facilities.

This is no small threat. Churches, synagogues, mosques and other religious centres are magnets for vote-seekers. Candidates depend on these connections, especially in many culturally diverse areas, like Surrey, a suburb south of Vancouver, where close elections can be won or lost.

This was a frightening development in Canadian politics. The immediate impact was to undermine what support I may have had within my caucus, particularly among my colleagues from ridings with significant Muslim populations. Their careers were now on the line. And since Surrey has 10 constituencies, many with significant Muslim communities and several of them swing ridings, a threat like this held the potential to throw a provincial election.

This certainly put the Premier and the party under pressure.

Even so, politics involves pressures. The test of leadership is managing the pressure and doing the right thing anyway.

I understood immediately the burden this ultimatum put on the Premier. And I knew, as he probably did, that his response to it would likely be his most serious test as leader so far. This entire controversy was about me, of course. But with the imams' letter, it shifted considerably to a larger issue of the role of religious leaders in a democracy and how an elected leader manages a situation in which a small group of influential community figures seeks to use coercion to exact political retribution.

Did it matter that the issue was Israel and Palestine and that the clergy making the threat were Muslim? What would the Premier's response have been, I wonder, had the issue been, say, reproductive freedom or LGBTQ+ rights and the clergy were Catholic bishops?

There would be quite a dogpile before this was over. It seemed everyone had an opinion on me.

Jagmeet Singh, the federal NDP leader, posted on Instagram: "The comments are not only factually wrong, but offensive and irresponsible. . . . At a time when we are facing increasing division in our country, elected leaders must be voices for peace and justice. . . . I have heard from many who were harmed by these comments, and I have discussed my serious concerns with Premier Eby."

This was a high horse for the NDP leader to be riding, given that his position on Israel and Palestine has advocated a one-sided, intolerant, anti-Israel narrative that polarizes Canadians and discourages the compromise and coexistence that might advance peace and justice in the Middle East.

A member of his caucus, Matthew Green, the NDP MP for Hamilton Centre, jumped into the fray, accusing me on X of an "oversimplification of such a deeply rooted and painful history" and said my appearance on the panel did "not contribute to the understanding or resolution of the conflict but rather exacerbates tensions and misunderstanding."

This would be a mouthful coming from anybody. But from Matthew Green, whose interventions on the issue of Israel and Palestine seem deliberately formulated to exacerbate tensions and epitomize oversimplification, insensitivity and misunderstanding, it was especially rich.

Comments like these were countered by kind messages from so many others. During this time, I received an enormous amount of support. I heard from people I had never heard from before—not only in British Columbia's Jewish community and in my riding, but from across Canada and from the United States. People sent me notes and emails, including quotes from Mark Twain's book *The Innocents Abroad*, in which he described his visit to Palestine in 1867, where he discovered "a blistering naked treeless land" that was "desolate and unlovely" and "untenanted by any living creature and unblessed by any feature that is pleasant." I'm no Mark Twain, clearly, because "crappy piece of land" is innocuous by comparison.

"You did nothing wrong" was the common message I received, as well as "You shouldn't have apologized." People even tried making donations to my campaign—I had to tell them I was not running again. I felt very touched. People sent me artwork and small gifts. A woman on Gabriola Island sent a card in which her friends and neighbours added their kind thoughts.

These messages and tokens of appreciation brought tremendous comfort. It was these notes, especially from non-Jews, that carried me through those moments when my world turned upside-down.

Nonetheless, Saturday dragged by. I called a friend for a walk to clear my head. I stayed off social media. It was the proverbial calm before the storm.

Sunday was pivotal. A major party fundraiser in Surrey was to bring hundreds of NDP supporters together but organizers cancelled it because a mob was threatening to storm the event.

On Sunday, I also received texts from some members of the Press Gallery suggesting that they had got it wrong on Friday. A few of them let me know that this was probably not going to blow over as quickly as they had thought.

Then the Premier called and asked me to attend the next day's caucus meeting only long enough to apologize to my colleagues for what he described as my breaching of our commitment to avoid commenting on the Israel-Gaza conflict. He said he felt that the caucus needed to have a conversation about my actions without me in the room.

I agreed with the idea of apologizing to my colleagues for what had become a firestorm, but this was my first clue that the Premier did not have my back anymore.

The order that I come, make an apology, not explain myself or what I meant, and leave was—*is*—a bizarre approach for a leader to take.

In counselling and other forms of healthy group interactions, dialogue and decisions take place with those affected in the conversation. The caucus discussion was to take place behind my back—and yet with my full knowledge. You never do that. If there is a problem in the group, you keep the person in the group. If someone is to be disciplined, you include them in the process, permit them to defend or explain themselves, and allow the group to discuss and decide, however difficult that conversation may be.

Instead, the Premier broke almost every rule of healthy group dynamics. He set it up so that everyone apparently had a vote on my future. This was especially odd. The Premier appoints his cabinet. Since when did caucus get to vote on who is in and who is out of cabinet? If this had been a discussion about ejecting me from caucus, it might have been appropriate to engage the entire group. But they weren't kicking me out of caucus, they were discussing my role in cabinet. Getting tossed from cabinet would still leave me a member of the caucus. How would I ever feel safe or comfortable in a caucus that seemed eager to have a discussion about me, without me?

The Premier set it up so I would be prevented from trusting anybody who had been in that room. I would never know what happened or what was said. Caucus confidentiality is always in play but, in this case, I suspect he ordered an extra level of muzzling because the cone of silence around what happened after I left has been almost total. All I know is that, according to a couple of colleagues, some people said really nice things about me. Lovely to know. But apparently not relevant to the outcome.

As I prepared to address the caucus meeting, the outrage that had consumed social media all weekend, topped the newscasts, and shut down the fundraiser continued in the form of masked protesters outside the caucus meeting, which took place at a Surrey hotel.

The Premier's Office had drafted a grovelling apology that I was to read to my colleagues. I was told not to explain what I had been trying to say. I was not to talk about what it was like for me, as a Jew, living in this time. I was to be humble, cautious and contrite. It was as though I was on trial and that my colleagues were the jury and the judge.

On Monday morning, my husband Dan drove me the few minutes' from our home in Coquitlam to the caucus meeting in Surrey. We tried to arrive a bit early to avoid the protesters, but they were already gathered. I ducked down in my seat so they couldn't see me. Our anxiety was high. The protesters were looking for me, screaming for my resignation.

We drove into the underground parking of the hotel. A member of the Premier's staff met us and ushered me through staff elevators and back hallways into the staff lunchroom so that I was out of sight of the protesters. I waited there for my time to read my apology. I was exhausted from lack of sleep, I hadn't eaten since Friday and was stunned at how the world had turned so quickly.

Eventually I got word that the caucus was ready for me.

This is what the Premier's staff wrote for me and what I read:

"My apologies to all of you about the comments while on a panel earlier this week. I am truly sorry to all of you for my completely offensive language. My words were an inappropriate way to describe the history of the Middle East, and they were never meant as any sort of commentary on the current conflict. Regardless of that, I know my comments have hurt a lot of people. They have also led to terrible claims about us as a caucus and as a government.

"I truly regret what I said. Please forgive me."

I felt set up. It was a show trial in which the outcome was never in doubt. The entire process was so humiliating and illegitimate that I could not look my colleagues in the eyes. I focused on the microphone.

I was forbidden from justifying in any way my error in language. Even so, I pushed back a little bit. I added a few words to the script. I used a tightrope metaphor, trying to explain the dual roles I was playing as a Jew and as a member of a government and a party that were increasingly proving to be hostile environments for Jews. My competing identities, as a Jew and as a New Democrat were becoming unsustainable.

Why did I play my part in this kangaroo court? In retrospect, I had no good options. I guess the eternal optimist in me still had hope that my colleagues would find the humanity to forgive, as they had forgiven the transgressions of my colleagues so many other times, including on this very topic. I was exhausted, worn down and going through the motions. I would certainly replay my choices again and again in my head—all my choices, including this apology. In the end, though, probably nothing on my part would have changed the outcome.

I maintain that what happened is not because of what I said, but because of who I am. And this is not something I can change.

I don't think my colleagues understood what it was like for me, as a Jew. Probably no cultural community has ever experienced a situation like what the Jewish community was going through at that moment. And this caucus—ostensibly progressive, social justice-minded, compassionate leaders committed to multiculturalism, inclusion and empathy—demonstrated no empathy for my situation. They seemed to have no comprehension of what the Jewish community was experiencing.

My colleagues, I think, had no idea the work I was doing to maintain the government's legitimacy within the Jewish community. Even if, as some colleagues clearly demonstrated, they didn't care about the Jewish community, this had larger implications. This affected the government's standing with the broader population because most British Columbians align more with the Jewish community and with Israel than they do with the radical extremists who are wagging the NDP dog on this issue. I was doing this absolutely alone. No one else in our government was standing up. No one.

As I stood at the microphone in that caucus meeting, I could feel the atmosphere in the room. There was precisely no appetite for anything from me but the pleading apology the Premier's Office instructed me to read. My mild effort to go off-script and explain myself was not going to alter the outcome, so I gave up.

As I walked toward the exit, some extended their hands to touch me, but I didn't feel comforted. I felt sad and betrayed. And I knew they would demand my resignation.

A member of the Premier's staff led me to her car and I again ducked down in my seat as we exited the underground parking.

There were more people gathered on the sidewalk outside the hotel. I remember thinking, *It's Monday morning, don't these people have to go to work?*

We got to my house, and I was told that the Premier would call me later. The person who drove me home would stay with me at the house as a point of contact with the Premier's Office. This was interesting. The Premier has my cell number. We have called each other plenty of times. Presumably, the idea was that, if the Premier called and I was on another call or otherwise unavailable, the staffer could intervene and connect me. More likely, the Premier's Office wanted to keep a leash on me, to make sure I didn't make any phone calls they didn't want me to make.

I returned to the 1,000-piece puzzle. I was too uneasy to do anything else. I still had no appetite.

Dan was doing his best to keep busy. This was killing him too and his desire to protect me from the vitriol and hatred was palpable. He checked on me regularly, urging me to eat, joining me at the puzzle table and trying to distract me with conversation. Even though I knew what the verdict would be, I was fully absorbed with dread and angst.

The Premier called me shortly after noon.

He told me that he could not "see a way forward." I asked him what that meant. He repeated the phrase. It seemed to me as though he had scripted his words, as if to avoid firing me and to position what was about to happen as me resigning.

For 10 years, I had been building a relationship between our party and government, and the Jewish community, and all of that was at risk if I were fired. Perhaps he thought he could get rid of me without harming relations with the Jewish community if I resigned.

I do not know if this was his strategy. Nor did I mention that my firing would look like capitulation to coercion from activist clergy or that it sent the message that radical extremists like those who forced the cancellation of our event the night before could get a minister fired if they hollered loud enough.

I told the Premier that if he wanted my resignation, I would give it to him, but he needed to ask for it.

In the end, he didn't fire me and I didn't resign, although the undeniable conclusion of the call was that I was no longer in cabinet. The Premier's Office was already at work on a news release.

I told them to make sure the release stated that the Premier asked me to step down. There were back-and-forth phone calls between me and the Premier's staff. He still seemed to refuse to take responsibility.

While I was arguing with the Premier's team on the press release, I received a text from my friend and colleague, Lisa Beare, MLA for Maple Ridge-Pitt Meadows and Minister of Citizens' Services. (She would become Minister of Post-Secondary Education after I was ousted.) Lisa asked me to answer my phone as she was going to call.

Over the years, a small group of women cabinet ministers became friends, checking in with one another. We served as sounding boards, we supported one another through tough times with our files, and we would get together a couple of times during a parliamentary session for a meal or a glass of wine. These friendships helped us juggle the demands of the job and our personal lives and we were able to commiserate and celebrate the twists and turns of political drama. These women were my friends—or I thought they were.

Lisa called to say that I really should resign. Presumably the Premier's Office wanted to erase any ambiguity about whether I was fired or resigned and so sent Lisa to get my head on a pike.

She explained that there were no other options and it would be best for everyone if I did the right thing.

*The right thing*? I was the one besieged by a mob and they wanted *me* to do the right thing?

And then came what felt like the ultimate betrayal. Lisa explained that if I resigned I could at least find my way back to cabinet at some point.

It felt bad enough that a friend would call to do the Premier's dirty work and pressure me to resign. A true friend might have taken a different tack and told the Premier to do his job and fire me. As strange as that sounds, it would have been the right thing to do in this morally inverted scenario. I was heartbroken that Lisa would call to ask for my resignation, but the suggestion that I could make my way back to cabinet was the line that really set me off.

She was insulting my intelligence. This was February. The election was in October. Lisa knew I was not seeking re-election. No one thought I would return to cabinet. Ever. What world would someone have to be living in to dangle such a preposterous incentive? It seemed to me that she was willing to tell me whatever she thought I needed to hear to make me do what the Premier wanted. Friends don't behave like that.

Later, I would come to conclude that the Premier or someone on his team had posited the ridiculous scenario that I might return to cabinet after a time in detention. I eventually heard from other colleagues who hinted that such a return had indeed been implied.

This was simply bizarre. No political leader would seriously consider rehiring a fired minister, who was not seeking re-election, just a few months before an election.

Perhaps it was the "faint hope" approach. If I were stupid enough to believe that I could be rehabilitated to cabinet, perhaps I would be on my best behaviour in the meantime and not make waves for the Premier. Maybe I would keep doing my job as the "Jew in the Crew" and keep the Jewish community from feeling betrayed by the Premier and the government.

As I listened to Lisa, I wondered if the Premier had asked for her help. I could imagine the scene. The Premier saying to a small group of cabinet members that I was not willing to "do the right thing." And the Premier then asking my friend Lisa to call or, more likely, because she really likes to be helpful, Lisa offering to use her powers of persuasion.

Perhaps more laughable than the idea that I would be reappointed to cabinet was the belief that I would ever want to be back in cabinet alongside colleagues who would so enthusiastically abandon and betray me and my community.

Amid the worst moments of my life, given everything swirling around me, Lisa's phone call stands out as one of the most painful memories.

Meanwhile, despite my emphatic insistence, the Premier's communications team put together a press release stating that I had offered my resignation, hoping perhaps that I would sign anything put before me. After all, just a couple of hours earlier, I had dutifully read the pleading apology they had written.

I refused. I felt it was important that the statement honestly acknowledge that the Premier asked for my resignation, which resulted in me offering it. I have always believed that a cabinet minister serves at the pleasure of the Premier, so if the Premier no longer wanted me to serve, then he needed to own it. It was not my desire to leave cabinet. It was his desire (and perhaps, in a weird perversion of parliamentary tradition, the desire of the caucus) that I no longer serve. I was extremely disappointed, not only for myself but for the province, that the Premier would not or could not exercise the basic leadership and the courage to simply yank off the bandage.

Tearing off a bandage is a crude analogy, but it seems apt. I was, in a sense, the Jewish dressing protecting an open wound in the government. When we finally agreed on the wording that would end my term in cabinet, I believe that what remained behind was a gaping laceration that undermined the Premier's legitimacy with Jewish British Columbians and anyone with moral clarity.

This was the first time the new Premier had fired a minister. If this pandemonium was how he handled a crisis, it indicated to me that perhaps the province would be in for a tumultuous time as well.

The Premier's communications team and I went back and forth until I suggested that the most I would accept is that it was a "joint decision." There were two of us making decisions. Therefore, it was jointly made.

I signed off on the press release and waited for the next phase of the nightmare to begin.

I was stunned and exhausted but, in a small way, I was relieved. After some of the most wrenching days of my life—and I have had some wrenching days—at least I knew my fate. The ordeal was at an end.

If I felt a sense of relief that it was over, I'm sure that the Premier's Office was relieved as well. Their relief came in the form of a text shortly after I hung up from my call with the Premier, when one of his staffers sent me the following message:

"Selina, I am so sorry. I can't imagine what you are going through. I am beyond impressed by your selflessness in all of this fucking shit."

This was interesting for a few reasons. It was very personal. Political staffers refer to cabinet members as "minister," not by their first names. This was an individual going out on a limb to reach out to me personally, which was gutsy and I appreciated it.

The larger, political message I took from this was that my act was considered a self-sacrifice for the team, not a justified firing based on a matter of principle. I was cut loose not because I had done anything wrong, but to stop the noise, to satiate the baying crowds and to bend to the coercion of a group of Muslim clergy.

My firing (or resignation, or joint decision) was not a matter of principle—on the contrary. This was capitulation to a very vocal group of people.

Meanwhile, I had no idea what transpired at the caucus meeting, what was said by the people whom I defended, worked with, and cared about. They had a conversation about me, without me. What did they say? Did anyone advocate for me? If so, who? Were there antisemitic remarks said aloud? If so, by whom? And the biggest question for me: How can I ever trust anyone who participated in this exercise? Yes, many sent me caring notes. Several of my colleagues sent me messages about how sorry they were about what happened. One person even acknowledged that I carried an extra burden, an apparent reference to the emotional weight I carried as a Jew in these times. But, in the end, what difference did any of this make? It meant nothing. It was the political equivalent of the proverbial thoughts and prayers. They did not support me when I needed them. None of this was in any way comforting. I felt betrayed. I was betrayed.

The only other whisper I heard about what went on in that meeting was that I was seen to have breached the commitment to not talk about the conflict between Israel and Hamas.

There is some irony here. I did not talk about the conflict. My words were in the context of how overseas events were impacting Jews and the discourse *in Canada, in British Columbia*. They accused me of breaching the prohibition, but I was talking about antisemitism, not about the conflict.

I had spent the previous four months since October 7 portraying our government and my colleagues as people the Jewish community could trust amid the greatest surge of antisemitism we have seen in generations. Now these people had turned on me—and by extension, on the Jewish community. I had been the government's voice in the Jewish community and the Jewish community's voice in the government, the "Jew in the Crew." That had positive impacts on both of my communities—but one side, the New Democrat side, broke the agreement. Collectively, they decided that I was no longer an asset to the government. I was now a liability.

Any parent will tell their kids it is important to learn lessons from failures or defeats. I learned something very important that day.

Many Jewish people are going through a sad process right now, in which we mentally file through the friends we think we might be able to rely on if history were to repeat itself and we had to go into hiding.

I learned that none of these people would hide me. Not the Premier, not my colleagues and not the people who claimed to be my friends.

That's a hard lesson to learn.

# *On Being a Jew*

I HAVE COME TO the conclusion that the outrage around my "crappy piece of land" comment was almost entirely manufactured. Like so much today, it seemed to be less about truth and what is right than seeing your perceived enemy get their comeuppance.

As part of my "deep work" I was to make phone calls to a number of community and organizational leaders. The Premier's Office provided me with a list. They had a staffer prepare what I was to say, the tone I was to take and they sat with me while I made these calls.

When I reached out to leaders in cultural communities to apologize and make amends for the words that the Premier insisted had caused such harm, some of the people I spoke with accepted my apology immediately. Others dismissed the whole thing as a tempest in a teapot. Some had no idea what I was talking about and I had to explain why I was calling. Of those who were genuinely angry about what I had said, not one could even remotely articulate how my words were hurtful.

That's a problem in this narrative.

I was told I had caused immense, almost irreparable pain. The "depth of work" I had to do to repair this egregious infliction of hurt, according to the Premier, was so vast that I couldn't possibly perform my tasks as Minister of Post-Secondary Education.

And yet, when I made call after call, asking forgiveness and probing to understand just what it was about my words that caused pain so that I could learn and avoid repeating the error, there was simply no explanation.

As a family counsellor, I know that emotions can be difficult to communicate. But the context of the pain I supposedly caused was not, for the individuals I was engaging with, so personal and devastating that they were unable to express their feelings. No, they didn't have those feelings to express.

Nobody genuinely thought what I said was Islamophobic. Nobody genuinely thought my words impugned Indigenous peoples in Palestine or in Canada. Nobody was actually harmed.

This was a *Gotcha!* to nab the most prominent Jew in cabinet. Those who brought me down still contend that these were deeply offensive words that caused such hurt. They insist I was brought down by my "racist" comments. But there is simply no standard or measure by which what I said could be interpreted as racist, Islamophobic or anything other than tactless.

It is my supposition that I was brought down because I'm a Jew.

This invites a different conversation.

There is a great deal of hair-splitting around this—and that has allowed too many, including most of my former colleagues, to remain silent in the face of antisemitism.

*I was not targeted because I am a Jew*, the argument goes. *I was targeted because I am a Zionist.*

And here is the nut of this discussion.

That is a false dichotomy. I am a Jew, so I am a Zionist. I am a Zionist because I am a Jew.

Yes, you can find non-Zionist and anti-Zionist Jews. They are easy to spot. Anti-Israel groups push them to the front of the queue to prove their cause is not antisemitic because *Look! Here's a Jew!* The word for this is tokenism.

Like the joke about how you can tell someone who is a vegan or people who do CrossFit: They'll tell you. Anti-Zionist Jews are extremely vocal, but this should not be mistaken as indicating that they are anything more than a tiny fringe group. A survey published in the spring 2024 edition of *Canadian Jewish Studies / Études juives canadiennes* indicates three percent of Canadian Jews are anti-Zionist.

These few, loud individuals are the exceptions that prove the rule. For the vast majority of Jews in Canada and around the world, Israel holds an almost inexpressible place in our hearts and souls. This is not always easy for Jews to articulate. It is especially difficult to articulate when we have people screaming in our faces.

The reason many non-Jewish Canadians do not understand the relationship between Jews and Israel is because we have not had this conversation. A small group of intolerant activists have rubbed salt in Jewish wounds and terrorized us every time we try to convey why Israel matters to us. Many of us have simply stopped trying to have these conversations. It is just too painful.

As a result, Canadians of goodwill, people who might listen to us and empathize, do not get the opportunity because many Jews have been driven out of the dialogue.

There is a great irony here, since it is precisely the intolerant activists who will tell you—any time we try to explain how Israel is central to our Jewishness—that *we* are silencing *them*. They shout at us: "Anti-Zionism is not antisemitism!" They behave as though every expression of concern about antisemitism is a plot aimed at them.

The additional irony here is that progressive, antiracist people would never dismiss any other group of people who say they are experiencing racism by responding *No you're not!* The activists' very defence is proof of their culpability.

This discussion demands nuance and that is something that our interlocutors not only refuse to engage in, but actively subvert and shut down.

The webinar that led to my firing is the perfect example. This was an opportunity for Canadian officials to dialogue and be heard on the serious issue of antisemitism. Not only does no one remember what was said aside from my Four Fateful Words. The mob managed to get the messenger fired for even attempting to speak about the problem. So who, after all, is silencing whom?

Complicating the dialogue we need to have is a complexity around the very definition of "Jew." Many people think "Jewish" is exclusively a religious identity. This is clearly the perspective of people who mistakenly think Israel is a "theocracy."

Jewishness is not simply a religion. Jews share a religious heritage, but we are not defined only by that. Jews are a community with a shared historical narrative, cultural expression, practices and traditions. Jews are an ethnocultural group, a people and a nation.

Judaism, the religion, is at the core of Jewishness, but Jewishness, the peoplehood, is something broader. You can be Jewish and an atheist. You can convert to Judaism and so be a Jew without being ethnically Jewish. A Jew can convert to another religion and still be ethnically Jewish. These realities make Jewishness different from other identities.

Because of this complexity, and a lack of understanding around it, we sometimes see people arguing with Jewish people over whether our self-definition is valid and whether our experiences with racism are authentic. If Jews do not fit in the boxes these commentators assign to "race," then their attacks on us cannot be "racism."

It is generally accepted, certainly by progressives, that it is the right of people to define our own identities. Decent people do not deadname or misgender trans individuals. We do not tell people of mixed heritage, Kamala Harris or Barack Obama, say, or anyone else, what racial category they fit into. As a matter of practice, progressives believe no one has the right to define for members of other groups what their identities are. And yet a great many people, including progressives, feel absolutely free to tell Jews who and what we are.

I should also clarify why I use the term "anti-Jewish racism" even though Jews are not a race. Most people no longer subscribe to 19th-century ideas of "race science." We recognize racial categories as social constructs, not scientific ones. But antisemitism "racializes" Jews (even if it often problematically racializes us as "white"), and so the term racism to describe antisemitism is absolutely correct. Antisemitism is a form of racism and needs to be treated that way.

The discussion of antisemitism as it intersects with anti-Zionism is more complicated. Zionism is the right of Jews to self-determination. Anti-Zionism opposes that right. Anti-Zionism is not about Israel's government, it is a rejection of the right of the Jewish *people* to self-determination. This is a form of antisemitism.

It is silly to suggest that everyone who criticizes Israel's government is an antisemite. However, it is equally silly to pretend that our ideas about the Jewish *state* are utterly unconnected to our ideas about Jewish *people*. There is an intersection. But we will never get through that intersection—and we will never be able to confront antisemitism—if we meet obstruction every time we try to have dialogue that acknowledges the sanctity of Israel in the Jewish experience.

Attempts to definitively segregate anti-Zionism from antisemitism are usually disingenuous. These phenomena are not the same thing, but they are related. To dismiss all anti-Zionism as antisemitic is incorrect and unhelpful. But to deny any connection is nonsensical. It rejects even the potential existence of a form of racism that demands to be addressed.

For our purposes now, let me just put it this way: A few years ago, on the eve of the anniversary of Kristallnacht, when someone threw a boulder through the window of Hillel House, the Jewish student centre at the University of British Columbia, was that an anti-Zionist boulder? Or was it an antisemitic boulder? Outcomes matter more than intent.

Do we really need to spend a lot of time arguing over nomenclature? When Jewish people are pleading for sensitivity and empathy, and in return are greeted with quibbling over definitions and accusations that we use "false allegations" of antisemitism to manipulate pity, this only adds to Jewish people's increasing feelings of isolation.

When Jews in Canada are hiding their identities, afraid of congregating in Jewish spaces and otherwise experiencing a level of intimidation and fear no one in this country should have to endure, what difference does it make what term we use for this? If people are living in fear, does it really matter whether it is because they are Jews or because they are Zionists?

This in no way detracts from, nor should it even impact upon, our attitudes toward what is happening in a war half a world away. Two things can be true at the same time. A tragic war is taking place. And a community of Canadians—Jews—are under siege.

In recent years, we have had admirable societal conversations around race, gender, indigeneity, reconciliation and a great range of topics. We have not had the conversation we need around antisemitism.

That is a conversation we desperately need to have.

I'll start.

## *What Israel means to Jews*

All decent people agree that firebombing synagogues is antisemitic and wrong. Likewise blatant, hateful antisemitic language. All people of goodwill condemn that.

The place where we get into disagreement is where most Jewish people recognize a problem and many non-Jewish people, it seems, do not. It is at the intersection of antisemitism and anti-Zionism. The only way around this topic is through it. So let's move right to the hard part.

I am an optimistic person—in fact I've been called a Pollyanna. I tend to see the world through rose-tinted glasses and I don't apologize for that. It has helped me find solace and hope where some others might not have been able to.

There are many older Jews, I know, who pass on cautions to the younger ones, warning against a false sense of security, stories of neighbours who seemed kind but turned into collaborators.

When I hear the first-person narratives of Holocaust survivors, what surprises me is not that there are a few who hold deep suspicions about non-Jews. It's that so many have managed to build a life that *isn't* circumscribed by distrust, fear and anger. This is a level of resilience I cannot imagine, but I admire.

Jewishness, despite being so deeply rooted in tradition, is remarkably future-focused. It is a tradition that venerates *this* life, not an afterlife. Jewish tradition commemorates and learns from the past, but mostly as a means for ensuring a better future.

Despite pogroms and genocides, so many survivors are remarkably forward-looking. It is, to me, a miracle of human resilience that Holocaust survivors could start anew, create families, build their lives and contribute so much to their communities. Rarely have I heard stories of people descending into irredeemable despondency after all they had witnessed and experienced. This is astonishing and inspiring to me. I have never faced a level of inhumanity like those survivors endured. Still, I know there are people who hate—I know it better now than ever—but I have a basic belief in human goodness.

I also, though, vehemently reject the offensive idea that Jews who harbour distrust of others are victims of a "persecution complex." They are not. They are students of history.

Jewish history is crowded with examples of Jews being welcomed, integrated and fully accepted in societies—in Europe, North Africa, the Middle East—until they weren't. And when they weren't, it came almost always like a bolt from the blue. It was, practically without exception, an uprising that seemed to emerge from nowhere at a time when the Jews in that place and time concluded that they were finally among people who would accept them. Only to find they were among people who would kill them—or who wouldn't kill them but who would point out their homes to the people who would.

My family fled Europe during the czarist pogroms around the turn of the 20th century, before the Holocaust, so I do not have a direct familial history with that cataclysm. Many Canadian Jews do, though.

The history of Vancouver's Jewish community, to use the example most familiar to me, has been profoundly impacted by the arrival of Holocaust survivors. Their immigration after the war, the families they started, the businesses they built, the Jewish community agencies they launched or strengthened all bear the indelible legacy of their worldview, resilience and philanthropy. Their imprints on our community include their sensitivities around subtle changes in social tolerance. This is not evidence of a "persecution complex." This is an appropriate human response to the world as it has been and as it is.

The immediate postwar era in Vancouver's Jewish community was a time of unprecedented growth. This was true in many communities because the postwar economies in North America represented the longest sustained economic expansion in human history. Everything was growing.

In the Jewish community, it was something more. The community invested in new, renovated and rebuilt institutions. Synagogues, day schools, community centres and organizations were built or expanded to accommodate the newcomers from Europe and the naturally growing community already here.

Whether those who were building the community at that time were entirely conscious of it or not, they were engaging in an act of profound revival both physical and spiritual. They may have been at the remote edge of a continent far away from the horrors of Europe, but the reality of what had happened there was immediate and adjacent.

Few of the survivors who came to Vancouver would speak much of their experiences for decades to come—many never did. But every Jew, even in this safe and distant place, understood that two of every three Jews in Europe had been murdered in just a few years. More than 90 percent of Jewish children who were alive in Europe in 1939 were dead in 1945, because the goal of the genocide was not only to kill the Jewish present but to kill the Jewish future. Of all the Jews in the world alive in 1939, one in three had been murdered by 1945. Those Jews who survived the war in Europe became refugees with nowhere to go.

We still feel these demographic impacts. Before the Holocaust, there were almost 17 million Jews in the world. Today, there are about 15.8 million Jews worldwide, about half of them in Israel.

The profound loss experienced in the Holocaust impacted every Jew and it was our collective responsibility to rebuild.

This is what every Jew, Canadian-born or recently arrived survivor, probably understood intuitively. And so, when they invested their money and muscle into building Jewish Vancouver, it was part of a larger renaissance. They were rebuilding the Jewish people.

At this same moment, in 1947, almost every Jew in the world held their breath as the new United Nations voted on whether to endorse a partition of the British colonial territory of Palestine into two states—a country for the Jewish people and a country for the Arab people of the area. When the vote passed, 33 to 13, with 10 abstentions, Jews worldwide erupted in jubilation.

As is so often the case in moments of Jewish celebration—like the breaking of glass at a wedding ceremony to commemorate the destruction of the ancient Jewish Temple in Jerusalem—a cloud of heartache existed amid the joy. Every Arab country rejected the partition. They were unanimously opposed to the idea of a Jewish state. They were threatening not just war but annihilation. The very language that had preceded the genocide that had just ended in Europe was now imported to the Middle East, where Jews had invested their collective hopes for redemption and security after almost 2,000 years of living as a stateless people at the whim of others, with tragic consequences century after century.

Even as Jewish Vancouverites threw themselves into building the infrastructure of our community and integrating the Holocaust survivors who came to our shores, they also devoted themselves to the building of the new Jewish state. Some Vancouverites travelled to Israel to fight in the war that everyone knew was coming. From selling the family silver to organizing bake sales, Vancouver's Jews of all ages, as Jews did worldwide, threw themselves into supporting the new state, which was born on May 14, 1948.

Within hours, the new country was attacked by the militaries of Egypt, Syria, Lebanon, Transjordan, Saudi Arabia, Iraq and Yemen.

Once again, Jews worldwide held their breath. Arab leaders, media and street rallies promised rivers of Jewish blood. Would there be a second genocide in less than a decade?

Not this time. At the cost of one percent of the total population of the country, Israel survived, and the war (if not the conflict) ended in July 1949.

Nothing could undo the loss and grief of the *Shoah*, the Holocaust. It would be entirely understandable for Jews to collectively plummet into a depth of despair from which they might never recover. Instead, even as the details of the unimaginable atrocities that occurred during the Holocaust became more widely known—not just the numbers of dead but the inconceivable physical and emotional brutalities that occurred—Jews resisted desolation. They turned attention, as we always have, to the future—to life, *l'chaim*.

Israel is the embodiment of Jewish hope after the Holocaust. This deep, collective investment is one reason that Israel is so central to so many. If people refuse to listen and to understand this centrality, they cannot understand how their words about Israel fall on Jewish ears. Israel is a testament to Jewish resilience and renaissance. It is a sacred trust for Jews.

The land of Israel, and the Jewish people's ancient and modern connection to it, is sacred, whether one is a religious Jew or not. Our identity is entwined with that land, its people and their security. For two millennia, Jews never stopped praying and hoping for redemption to the land from which the imperial Roman authorities expelled us 2,000 years ago. And even though we were expelled en masse, we have always retained a presence on those lands—the archaeology is undeniable. Zionism is, for all intents, an ancient indigenous land claim. And it is not an injustice but a fulfilment of justice that we have redeemed our people and our land.

Most early Zionists idealized Jews coexisting with their neighbours and it was Arab intransigence—not Jewish self-determination—that started this conflict.

But it is important to understand that this sacred, ancient connection is not all that Israel means to Jewish people.

Israel is not *just* one thing or another.

It is not *just* our collective, tragically belated promise of security to the six million who were murdered, though it is that.

It is not *just* a deterrent to future genocides by ensuring there is a collective Jewish defence, though it is also that.

It is not *just* the ancient homeland of the Jewish people redeemed in our lifetimes as the modern incarnation of Jewish peoplehood, though it is that.

It is not *just* the land where every aspect of Jewish tradition is rooted, from the spring agricultural festivals to the autumn harvests that define the Hebrew calendar, though it is also that.

It is not *just* the embodiment of the Jewish commitment to survival in the face of all odds, even in the aftermath of the most nearly successful of many, many attempts to erase the Jewish people from the world, though it is that too.

And so much more.

To almost every Jew, Israel means something personal and profound, if almost inexpressible.

Even anti-Zionist Jews are deeply tied to this land. The opposite of love is not hate, said the late Holocaust survivor and Nobel laureate Elie Wiesel, it is indifference. If you have ever spoken with an anti-Zionist Jew, whether their opposition is theological, like some Hasidic ultra-Orthodox groups, or ideological, like the Jews who anti-Israel groups push to the front as tokenistic proof that antisemitism is not their accelerant, what you will never hear is indifference.

Israel holds a hallowed place in the heart of almost every Jew, and it rightly evokes visceral feelings, regardless of our religious, geographic, cultural or other identities.

This is what activists spit on when they spit on Israel. This is why Jews take deeply personal offence when our people's legitimate rights and connections to that land are attacked—and this is true even for Jews who have never set foot on that land.

## *Anti-Zionism and antisemitism*

The vehemence with which Israel is condemned—as much as the content of the attacks—convinces many Jews that something irrational is at play. The obsessive attention to this one conflict, and the rage Israel evokes even when it is not engulfed in war as it is now, is not commensurate with the range of conflicts, humanitarian concerns and other crises in the world. I suspect it has something to do with the fact that this conflict involves Jews.

In response, "pro-Palestinian" activists accuse us of using "false accusations of antisemitism" to silence criticism of Israel. But the accusations are not false. Antisemitism is rampant in the anti-Israel movement and simply repeating the mantra "Anti-Zionism is not antisemitism" does not negate that truth. The very phrase should offend progressive people because it dismisses even the potential existence of racism, and that's not how we deal with concerns like that.

More problematically, the idea that anti-Zionism is hermetically detached from antisemitism is belied, if nothing else, by history. The genesis of anti-Zionism was, quite simply, antisemitism.

Unanimous opposition to the existence of Israel by the Arab world, in 1947, and the attempts to annihilate Israel in 1948 and 1967, were not premised on complicated geopolitical considerations, or any of the other issues we think of as central to this conflict, like the occupation, settlements, refugees or "right of return." Remember—none of those things existed in 1947 or 1948, but the opposition to the existence of a Jewish state was unanimous at that time among Arab and Muslim-majority countries.

That opposition originated and remains premised at its absolute core on opposition to the idea that Jewish people have a right to national self-determination in our ancestral land. That's the genesis and the heart of anti-Zionism.

That anti-Zionism's origin story is unequivocally antisemitic does not mean people who criticize Israel's government today are necessarily or irredeemably antisemitic. And there are plenty of reasons to criticize Israeli policies and leaders, as there are to criticize any government. Criticizing Israel's government is not antisemitism.

But the mantra "Anti-Zionism is not antisemitism" is demonstrably false because anti-Zionism was born of antisemitism. A raft of justifications has been laid out across the decades. But the simple truth is this: Arab opposition to the Partition Resolution was based on the Arab states refusing to tolerate a self-determined Jewish people living in the Middle East.

Actions of the Israeli government and military have made it easy to condemn Israel. But the heart of this conflict has always been an antisemitic, xenophobic, intolerant refusal to accept Jews in a land that most Muslim leaders contend is theirs and must not be shared.

Despite this fundamentally racist foundation, or perhaps to distract from it, the anti-Israel narrative has evolved to depict Israel as something it is not. There has been a massive distortion of history and a near-total inversion around who is perceived as the indigenous people of this land, and a fictionalized narrative of sins has been created to depict Israel as irredeemably wicked.

Certain anti-Zionist tropes, such as "colonialism" and "imperialism," simply fail by definition. Israel represents one of the greatest cases of postwar decolonization. If Israel were "imperialist," it would require a metropole—some distant power controlling the area.

In the narrative, of course, that power is "Western imperialism," a form of imperialism that is figurative, rather than literal. But even to make this assertion fit would require forcing a square peg into a round hole. Israel is the embodiment of an independent Jewish people and accusing it of being the Trojan horse of some external force has resonance in centuries of libels about Jewish people not being who we claim to be, being the puppet-masters of some larger nefarious plot, or acting as agents of an evil scheme.

Zionism can also not reasonably be accused of being colonialist, because Jews are the indigenous peoples in that land. Jerusalem is a Jewish city. The land that is now Israel was the Jewish homeland centuries before Islam was created and before Arabs migrated there from Arabia. While there has been an unbroken presence of Jews in that land, it is true that most Jews were expelled 2,000 years ago. However, this history, and the fact that other peoples moved into this territory in the interim, does not negate the Jewish claims to our ancestral lands. That is not how indigeneity works.

Among other tropes that need dismantling is the "apartheid" libel.

Governments that can be said to resemble apartheid do exist, but they are not in Israel. Gender apartheid is rampant across the region. Racial and national categorizations of people—including in Arab states that refuse to grant citizenship to Palestinian refugees (or their children, or their grandchildren or their great-grandchildren)—could reasonably be compared to apartheid. The dehumanization of half the population of Afghanistan—the female half—who are treated less like humans without rights than like inanimate possessions, far more resembles apartheid than even the most fevered allegations against Israel.

Ultimately, none of these arguments—including who was there first—should really matter. Believing that Israel is the embodiment of apartheid, imperialism, colonialism, that it is a "religious ethnostate," or whatever other counterfactual argument we want to throw at it will not free Palestine or alleviate the suffering of the people in the region.

Israel is not going anywhere. Until Palestinian leaders and their allies recognize and accept this—and adopt a political program that finally accepts an independent Palestine *alongside of*, not *instead of*, Israel—there will not be an independent Palestine.

Coexistence is the only way to free Palestine. Every time people chant "From the river to the sea," an independent Palestine is pushed further away.

The only path to peace and Palestinian self-determination is negotiation. Every act of intolerance harms these goals. Extremism entrenches some Israelis and their allies into a certainty that the world is against them and therefore military power is more necessary than ever. This justifies Israeli intransigence. It rewards terrorism and encourages Palestinian leaders and others to believe that the world supports continued violence and the destruction of Israel. This will never lead to a free Palestine.

Every act and statement demonizing Israel makes it more difficult for Palestinian leaders to sit down with Israeli negotiators because the more Israel is demonized, the more negotiations leading to a two-state solution become akin to making a deal with the devil.

Here is the bottom line: If we are not advancing a future of shared peace and coexistence, we are advancing a future of continued war and conflict.

It is worth noting that both Israelis and Palestinians have been victimized by those masquerading as their allies. This is a lesson that "pro-Palestinian" activists would do well to learn.

Israel was not created, as some people suggest, as an act of benevolence by a post-Holocaust world. No one "gave" Israel to the Jews. The United Nations General Assembly voted for a Jewish state and an Arab state in Palestine and then abandoned the Jews to defend their new state against an armed onslaught by all their neighbouring countries' armies who explicitly promised annihilation.

Western countries voted for the Partition Resolution less out of benevolence than out of self-interest. Canada, the United States and the other nations that turned their backs on the Jews before the war were no more welcoming of the surviving remnant of European Jewry after the war. For them, Israel was a faraway place to resolve the problem of Jewish refugees. Once they had cast their votes at the UN, they abandoned the Jews again to enemies promising genocide.

The Palestinian case is massively different, of course, but also involves betrayal by supposed friends.

Arab leaders have exploited and abused the Palestinian people for generations. It was the Arab League that made the decision on behalf of Arab Palestinians to reject the Partition Resolution. That fateful act made the Palestinians a stateless people. The Arab League's subsequent rejection, at Khartoum in 1967, of Israel's offer of the Palestinian Territories in exchange for nothing but a promise of peaceful coexistence was again made not by Palestinians but by their "friends" in the Arab League. That decision solidified Palestinian statelessness for another six decades and counting.

The Arab states' leaders, and as time progressed the tyrants and dictators of the broader Muslim world, saw the value of a stateless, oppressed Palestinian people as a welcome distraction for their own oppressed citizens. The Palestinian problem has served as a valuable diversion to redirect legitimate rage away from Arab and Muslim oppressors and toward that most time-tested of scapegoats, Jews. Or, as the scapegoat now manifests, the Jewish state.

Perpetuating Palestinian statelessness, not resolving it, is in the interest of dictators across the Middle East and North Africa. Overseas activists play a role in this inhumane scheme by rewarding this conspiracy of statelessness. When they chant "Free Palestine!" they do so ignorant of the reasons why Palestine is not free—and whose interests that statelessness serves.

The Western world supported the idea of a Jewish state because it suited their objectives of resolving the Jewish refugee problem without taking any responsibility themselves. Nevertheless, Israelis took the opportunity they were given and built a new society that deserve emulation, not condemnation.

The Arab and Muslim states—with the exception of Egypt and Jordan and more recently the signatories of the Abraham Accords—have prevented coexistence between Israel and its neighbours, which is the only route by which peace and Palestinian self-determination will emerge. They have prevented the creation of a Palestinian state. This suits the objectives of Arab and Muslim autocrats because the obsession with the Palestinian-Israeli conflict deflects attention from their governments' own bad behaviours.

We must advance a situation where the needs and interests of the Palestinian and Israeli peoples are placed above the needs of other forces with their own agendas.

That is a geopolitical imperative that is well beyond the scope of this book. However, it is not entirely unrelated, because what Canadian activists are doing too often is placing their own needs above the well-being of the people for whom they claim to be allies.

Those who truly want a free Palestine need to be advancing coexistence, not a Palestine "from the river to the sea." They need to be condemning Hamas, not rewarding them. They must act in ways that bring Israelis and Palestinians together, rather than encouraging continued conflict, which is what "pro-Palestinian" activists in Canada have been overwhelmingly engaged in since October 7, 2023.

All of this is premised on the idea that Canadian activists are having any substantive impact on events *over there*. While I believe strongly in the power of individuals to make change in the world, we really should be honest about our limitations. All the activism we are seeing on campuses and in the streets in Canada and around the world is having limited effects on Israelis and Palestinians.

What these activists are undeniably having an impact on is the atmosphere *over here*. And there is almost nothing constructive or positive about that.

## *Will Canada remain safe for Jews?*

Some Jewish Canadians are, for the first time, questioning whether we have a future in this country. Yes, it has come to this. We have heard the stories from just two generations ago of the European aunts and uncles who vacillated, wondering how long they should wait, hoping that things would get better and certain they couldn't get worse.

Jewish Canadians are now wondering if Canadian campuses are safe places for our kids and grandkids—and if campuses today are not safe, will the larger society be safe in future? And how long should we wait to find out?

It is not only the history of the Holocaust that infuses Jewish Canadians' sensitivities to the speed with which our position in a society can deteriorate. There is an entire other history that hardly any Canadians seem to know. In the second half of the 20th century, almost every country across North Africa and the Middle East was ethnically cleansed of Jews.

In 1948, there were more than 850,000 Jews living in that region, many who could trace their roots back centuries or, in the case of Iraq, millennia. Today, excluding Israel, there are about 4,000 Jews in that entire vast area of the world, almost all of them in Morocco and Tunisia. This constitutes one of the most enormous ethnic cleansings in human history—and it is almost entirely unknown to non-Jews.

We might say that the second half of the 20th century was as dangerous for Jews in the Middle East and North Africa as the first half of that bloody century was for Jews in Europe. The difference is that one single country now exists with an open-door policy for imperilled Jews.

Of course, the existence of a Jewish state does not guarantee Jewish security, as October 7 demonstrated. The Islamic Republic of Iran is developing nuclear weapons with the explicit goal of wiping Israel from the face of the earth. But a Jewish state, which is forced by history and geography to maintain one of the most powerful militaries in the world, remains the surest bet for Jewish collective security.

And yet, despite all these threats, despite the murder of six million Jews a mere 80 years ago, despite the ethnic cleansing of almost every Jew from every Muslim-majority country, despite the calls for annihilation from across many in the Arab and Muslim world and the chants of "From the river to the sea" on Canadian campuses and elsewhere, the world insists that Jewish people are overreacting. The world insists such atrocities couldn't happen again.

Jews and many non-Jews have been experiencing the world differently since October 7. Too many people, especially progressive people, have not taken the time to understand how their words impact on Jewish ears. Too many people are chanting when they should be listening.

Phrases that too many people seem to accept as harmless are heard by Jews as an explicit call for genocide or, at a minimum, as nonchalance about Jewish lives.

The rhetorical hair-splitting about terms like "From the river to the sea," "intifada," "resistance," "by any means necessary" and other language used in the "pro-Palestinian" discourse is especially jarring to Jews. Academic debates about whether this term or that phrase is *actually* a call to *literally* kill me and my family is a sign we have already gone over the edge of acceptable discourse.

Jews don't need elaborate instruments to gauge whether this rhetoric meets the standard of antisemitism. The fact that many of our neighbours seem satisfied that Jews really have nothing to worry about, no matter how incendiary the verbal attacks, is all the reason we need to worry.

This is why it was the silence of the vast majority of my colleagues that truly broke my heart. It was not the insensitive, hurtful words of the few. It was not so much that hateful and violent extremists might come for me and my family. It is that I no longer believed that those I thought I could depend on would hide me if the extremists did come for us.

It is more basic than this, though.

Israel is home to half the world's Jews and is a place to which almost every Jew in the world feels a deep, abiding connection. When the Jewish state is condemned in the most violent language humans can invent, demonized in ways that bear no connection to rational discourse, and subjected to condemnations that are orders of magnitude greater than those reserved for the worst human right offenders in the world, Jewish people recognize that for what it is.

We can criticize Israel's government and policies. But Jewish people view Israel as the national embodiment of our people.

So the guardrails anti-Israel activists think they are steering within—insisting that "Anti-Zionism is not antisemitism"—are largely irrelevant. To aim this level of irrational loathing not at specific behaviours or policies but at the existence of the country itself is felt by Jews—correctly—as an assault on our right to exist as a people.

The "pro-Palestinian" mobs, while larger than we like to see mobs, make up a comparatively small proportion of the Canadian population. Opinion polls indicate that most Canadians are not on the side of these extremists. And yet, we do not see adequate vigilance against antisemitism.

Police statistics, news reports, personal testimonies and self-reporting mechanisms indicate that intimidation, threats and violence against Jewish people and institutions in Canada are at levels unseen in generations. And too many Canadians—including my former colleagues—don't say or do anything.

What explains this indifference? How can so many Canadians—including, if not especially, those who consider themselves antiracist—dismiss all this evidence as nothing to get worked up over?

When things calm down *over there*, they seem to believe, things will calm down *over here*. But that is both strategically and morally wrong.

This much is true: Every time the conflict there flares up, the conflict here in Canada follows. But while there may be causal relationships, we must not misinterpret the relationship.

This cannot be stressed enough: We must reject the idea that conflict *here* is only a result of conflict *there*. That is an excuse for bigotry. Antisemitic threats, rhetoric and violence here are a consequence of pre-existing strains in our own society. External events are a pretext that lead some Canadians to act out in antisemitic ways.

We need to take responsibility for a Canadian problem and not pretend it is a foreign problem. When synagogues are firebombed in Vancouver, when Jewish-owned businesses in Toronto are attacked, when shots are fired at Jewish schools in Montréal, that is antisemitism and it is happening in Canada. It is inappropriate to cast blame or excuses anywhere else.

Most other overseas conflicts do not cause systematic attacks on ethnocultural groups in Canada, why does this one?

Antisemitism in Canada is not a manifestation of the grief about people killed and injured in a foreign war. We are all heartbroken about the loss of innocent lives. But setting fire to religious institutions in Canada is not a legitimate response to tragedies overseas. And yet, there seems to be an assumption that such acts of violence in Canada are not as serious as other forms of racist attacks because they relate to foreign events.

A conflict is no longer foreign when it threatens Canadians. We cannot treat antisemitism here as a by-product of war abroad.

Something else we seem determined to ignore is that violent acts are related to incendiary words. Progressive, antiracist activists recognize this in every other instance. When it comes to the inflammatory anti-Israel hyperbole that is everywhere in Canada right now and the parallel spike in anti-Jewish attacks, we have an obligation to acknowledge that connection and tamp down the level of rhetoric.

Instead, even those who proudly self-define as antiracist are not exercising caution or sensitivity, but pouring fuel on the already blazing inferno. This is an extraordinarily dangerous scenario. When we Jews draw attention to this reality, we are accused of trying to "silence" criticism of Israel.

This is just one example of how Jews are accused of mischaracterizing legitimate political activism as antisemitism, of pathologizing completely reasonable language. Let me explain how things that might be hypothetically defended as legitimate political expression sound to me like antisemitism.

For more than a year, we have heard chants of "Intifada! Revolution!" "From the river to the sea" and even "Long live October 7!"

To my ears—to almost every Jewish ear, I suspect—these are calls to kill Jews. That's antisemitism.

"Intifada," no matter what hedging those chanting it might tell you, is an overt call for violence against Jews. That's antisemitism in its purest form.

"From the river to the sea" is a call to eliminate the State of Israel and to make half the world's Jews—seven million people—stateless. Even if the 20th century had not demonstrated the catastrophic potential of Jewish statelessness, this would still sound to me like antisemitism.

When people support self-determination for Palestinians and all or most other groups, but not for Jews, I see antisemitism.

When I see people who take little to no interest in foreign affairs, but make this conflict and the blaming of Israel their foremost political cause, I suspect antisemitism.

When the federal NDP brings a motion to Parliament to cut off Canada's already insignificant military trade with Israel, I see that as an attempt to ensure that Israel is unable to defend its citizens from genocidal murderers. That's antisemitism.

I could go on. My point, though, is that things one person hears one way can be heard very differently by others.

The larger issue here is that, even if you think I'm overreacting, that doesn't mean there isn't a problem. Even if you think my definitions of what constitutes antisemitism are too liberally drawn, that does not alter the reality that many Canadians are not taking antisemitism seriously enough. Even if my definitions of antisemitism aren't the same as yours—even if we measure only by the strictest literal interpretation, such as police records of *actual physical attacks* against Jewish people and institutions—this is a problem that deserves more attention than we are devoting to it.

Instead, there seems to be a tendency among some people to assume that Jewish people are crying wolf.

Let's address that head on. Let's say that crying wolf does occasionally happen.

If this is happening, it is a comparatively minor offence when compared with the alternative, which is unequivocally happening. Overstating the problem of racism may occasionally occur—and there always seem to be a few who revel in identifying and highlighting these exceptional instances. But isn't *understating* racism, or even denying it, a greater offence?

Yes, it is possible that some Jews and others occasionally use the word "antisemitism" when maybe the situation doesn't fit the narrow definition. But what is a far more egregious affront to social justice, antiracism and human decency than sloppily employing a term like antisemitism is nitpicking over terminology rather than racing to the side of a victimized community.

There remain many who refute my insistence that I was a victim of antisemitism. No, I have been told, I was rightfully punished for ill-chosen (or racist, or otherwise offensive) words. Anti-Jewish animus was not the major factor in what happened and my attempts to project that are a devious, self-serving tool.

I am cautious when employing the term "antisemitism." But if I use the term "antisemitism" when some don't think it applies, maybe people should take a moment and ask themselves whether they would question a member of any other group when they use a particular term to describe their experiences. Instead of rushing to refute my characterization of what I experienced as antisemitism, isn't it always the appropriate response of progressive or antiracist people to first listen to why I feel this way?

Canadians in recent years have often done some of the difficult work around unlearning racism, recognizing white privilege and the legacy of white supremacy, addressing deep-seated biases around gender and sexuality. Our national conversation around truth and reconciliation has been inadequate, but it is happening.

Canadians have not begun the work we collectively have to do around antisemitism. Instead, we are arguing over definitions, denying it exists and accusing Jews of making mountains out of molehills. We have been doing basically everything *except* what we are supposed to do when confronted with so much as the potential that racial bias is influencing our approach to a cultural group.

Jewish people also have a responsibility to educate about this. In antiracist circles, we warn against placing the emotional labour on members of the affected community. At the same time, we know that advances in women's equality have come in part from men listening to the women in their lives. Progress in gay rights has come from our queer family members coming out and humanizing their experiences. Fighting racism is empowered when people of colour share their stories and when their friends and allies understand more deeply our biases and undertake to unlearn them.

Meeting Jews and listening to our experiences and perspectives is an important way to fight antisemitism. But there is a geographic and demographic problem.

Jews make up less than one percent of Canada's population—and almost all Canadian Jews live in Toronto and Montréal. A much smaller number live in Vancouver and the rest of us are scattered across the country.

Even if you do know some Jews, I'll let you in on a secret. They may not feel comfortable opening up to you.

Jews have learned from experience that opening ourselves up is often an invitation to hurt. Never has this been more true than in the months since October 7, 2023, when almost every Canadian Jew has been living in a parallel universe of pain.

That's what this book is about.

But this book is also a small attempt to address a problem that is exacerbated by the fact that many Canadians do not know any Jews.

By telling my story, one of the things I hope to do is make readers more familiar with Jewish people. I hope my personal story will make you feel like you know at least one Jewish person.

## *Walking a Tightrope*

WITHIN HOURS OF the October 7 attacks, Vancouver's Jewish community organized a vigil for people to come together, to deal with our grief and demonstrate solidarity with victims, survivors, the kidnapped and affected families. We were drawn there because each of us needed support. We needed to be among people who shared our heartache.

Many in the BC Jewish community have family or friends living in Israel. The family of Ben Mizrachi, a 22-year-old medic from Vancouver, was unable to contact him. They knew that he had been attending the Nova music festival, from which the grisliest imaginable images were emerging. It would be days before they found out for sure that he was among the murdered. We would later discover that he died a hero, returning to the scene of thc massacrc to try to save the lives of others.

Even if we do not have direct personal or familial connections to the victims, we felt this deeply. I know some people who, when asked "Do you have family in Israel?" respond, "Yes, I have millions of brothers and sisters there."

At the time of the vigil, the Premier was travelling on a long-planned tour. He asked me if he should alter his plans and come to Vancouver for the event. I let him know that I could represent the government, with the support of a number of our colleagues. I would bring condolences from him, and there would be future opportunities for him to be present for the Jewish community.

October 7 was the Saturday of the Thanksgiving weekend, so when I put out the call to my colleagues to join with the Jewish community on October 10, I knew not everyone was paying attention to their emails. I heard back from three or four colleagues.

The Legislature was not in session during Thanksgiving week and so some colleagues were out of town. Still, I was surprised at the lack of response. Most New Democrat MLAs represented Lower Mainland and Fraser Valley ridings. I messaged our Caucus Executive Director and asked for her help in reaching out to our MLAs to make sure we had a good showing of government representatives at the vigil. She sent an email underscoring my request for solidarity—and that did not get much response either.

Thankfully, two MLAs from Vancouver Island joined six of us from the Lower Mainland. Yet, out of a caucus of more than 50, of whom more than half live in Metro Vancouver, eight New Democrat MLAs standing with the Jewish community in our darkest moment in generations was a deep disappointment to me. I was embarrassed and hurt by how few of my colleagues made the effort to demonstrate support for this heartbroken community—my community. I reported back to the Premier about my distress. He acknowledged my concern and reassured me that he would remain a reliable ally.

As leaders, we knew that British Columbian Jews would be looking to us to calm their fears and ensure they were safe. And fears for physical and emotional safety were well-founded, from the earliest hours of this crisis.

While the official community vigil took place on the Tuesday at Jack Poole Plaza in downtown Vancouver, an ad hoc vigil at the Vancouver Art Gallery on Monday afternoon provided a taste of what our community would face in the months to come. As Jewish British Columbians grieved and prayed, a small cluster of people wearing keffiyehs and waving Palestinian flags, kept apart from the Jewish group by police, shouted and taunted the mourners. They were jubilant, celebrating the loss of Jewish lives just hours earlier.

This was a new level of antisemitic inhumanity that I do not think had been seen in Canada before.

There had not been, to be clear, any Israeli military response by this point. There was no plausible deniability that these protesters were doing anything other than rubbing salt in the wounds of Jewish people who were devastated by the news from Israel. Soon enough, we would see social media comments and hear much more from these protesters and others around the world rejoicing in the atrocities with which we were still coming to terms.

At this point, I was still prepared to give the benefit of the doubt to my caucus colleagues. Within days, though, the first unavoidable signs emerged that I would not find among some of them the basic compassion I would expect from people who imagine themselves to be progressive advocates of social justice.

My email asking colleagues to join me at the vigil did elicit some belated responses. Unfortunately, they were not what I had hoped.

Aman Singh, then-MLA for Richmond-Queensborough, who didn't reply to my invitation or attend the vigil, got around to responding two days after the community event. On Thursday, he hit "reply all" and suggested that caucus send out a press release supporting the Palestinian community.

Only five days had passed since the massacre of almost 1,200 civilians, most of them Jewish, and the rape, torture and kidnapping of hundreds of others. Had he not seen the carnage? Did he not witness the same brutality that I saw perpetrated by Hamas? Israelis were still assessing the impacts of the massacre, identifying body parts, scouring cars, homes and fields for human remains. We all knew war was coming and, as a result, the people of Gaza would suffer. But could he not even pause for a moment, out of basic human respect, to feel the pain of Jews in his community, even in his caucus?

No, without uttering a whisper of sympathy for murdered Jews, he leapfrogged right over those dismembered bodies to focus on what might happen in the future.

Katrina Chen, then-MLA for Burnaby-Lougheed, also jumped into the email chain supporting Aman's request. Again, not even a pause for the atrocities we just witnessed.

I was overwhelmed by anger and pain. Colleagues I had worked with, who I thought shared my values, gave not a moment of reflection for Jewish victims. The message I got from these colleagues was that the Israeli victims got what they deserved.

In a world where an October 7 could happen and people in my own city would gather to *celebrate* those atrocities, who could I and other Jewish people depend on if things deteriorated further right here at home? If elected officials of a progressive government seem untroubled by the mass murder of Jews in Israel, how could I depend on them as allies, as colleagues, as friends? If, God forbid, it came to that, how could I depend on them to hide me?

I went to that same dark place that many Jews went: *Never again is now.*

I texted the Premier. I told him I could not have the conversations that needed to take place with these colleagues.

"I need my colleagues right now to defend me and my family and I don't think I can count on several of them," I told the Premier.

I soon received a text message from Aman, who I suspect had heard from the Premier.

"Wanted to reach out," Aman wrote. "You have seen my email. I want you to know, which I think you already do, that I am and always have been a big supporter of the Jewish community and the people of Israel. And I understand that you have family there and I can't imagine how stressed out and worried you must be and my heart goes out to you. But I was also disturbed by the rhetoric of attack and now the reality of civilians being punished for what Hamas did. And to be clear what they did was absolutely horrific and they should be brought down. Seeing what is happening is breaking my heart. I wanted us as a caucus to recognize the pain in Gaza as well."

I later got a message from the Premier:

"Don't sweat this," he wrote. "I will sort it. Team finding time for us to chat."

And we did chat. I thanked the Premier, telling him I got a message from Aman, though it was an explanation, not an apology. The Premier seemed annoyed that Aman didn't apologize. However, that appeared to be the end of that particular drama. It was, however, a foreshadowing of things to come.

* * *

I checked in with a number of BC's Jewish community leaders pretty much every day in those first few weeks. I wanted to support them as they tried as best they could to support our community. They were our government's eyes and ears. I felt a significant responsibility to ensure that our government was listening and responding to the needs of a community that was struggling.

I also let the Premier know that this was a difficult time for me personally. He asked if he could share this at a caucus meeting, and of course I consented.

Given the experience with Aman and Katrina, I chose not to attend that particular caucus meeting because I did not want to risk hearing tactless comments from colleagues—it just would have been too difficult for me.

I was grateful that the Premier delivered this message, and I had hoped that it would keep my colleagues from adding to my distress and the challenges that came with walking a tightrope between supporting the Jewish community and being part of a government caucus and a political party that I could no longer deny contained a vein of deeply problematic insensitivity to Jewish suffering.

The Premier met with Jewish community leaders, including principals from Jewish day schools. He invited me and George Heyman, then-MLA for Vancouver-Fairview and Minister of Environment, to the meeting.

George, whose Jewish parents escaped occupied Poland and whose riding included the oldest and largest Orthodox synagogue in Vancouver, has had a challenging relationship with the Jewish community. For a number of reasons, many Jews have not seen George as an ally. For 10 years, I worked with George and the community to mend fences and we could see the fruits of our labour. George was at the table demonstrating his concern for the Jewish community.

The Premier listened intently and was struck by a story that Emily Greenberg, Principal of Talmud Torah Elementary School, shared with us. She described how, since October 7, she and other female faculty wore running shoes to school. She explained that they were all thinking the same thing: *I may need to be able to grab the students and run.*

I know this story impacted the Premier because he shared it publicly several times. He wanted to demonstrate that he understood the impact of the Hamas massacre on the Jewish community in BC.

That was the only meeting between the Premier and the Jewish community that I am aware of until March 2024, after the Premier asked for my resignation. That was fine—I was the Jew in the Crew. I had taken on the role of the government's liaison to the Jewish community in the intervening months and I was glad to do it.

In the following days, though, things became more challenging. Palestinian-Canadians were now also getting news from overseas as the Israeli military launched the ground offensive that we all knew was coming. Over the succeeding months, we would watch with heart-breaking grief as more innocent lives were lost.

As things began to escalate in Gaza, so did the hate towards Jews in Canada. In addition to a tsunami of online hostility, we started witnessing Molotov cocktails thrown at Jewish institutions, protests against Jewish-owned businesses, vandalism and hateful graffiti across the country, and vitriolic denunciations everywhere. There were regular anti-Israel demonstrations at the Vancouver Art Gallery and on the front lawn of the BC Legislature.

I was getting emails from Jewish British Columbians concerned about the rising hate.

I was hearing from people in the BC public service, provincial government employees whose colleagues were sporting keffiyehs and putting Palestinian flags in their shared workspaces and in their email signatures. I heard from an employee who was in a meeting where a First Nations land acknowledgement was expanded to include Palestinians.

Would these sorts of things have been OK if these had been, say, Ukrainian flags and symbols? Maybe, or maybe not. This is not apples to apples. I simply don't believe these were acts of good faith. Regardless of whatever guidelines exist for provincial government officials to express political opinions, I suspect the keffiyehs and other Palestinian symbols were deliberately intended to goad and intimidate Jewish colleagues. The Ukrainian example fails also, of course, because to display a Ukrainian flag is to stand for the territorial integrity of a sovereign country. To display a Palestinian flag, in the post-October 7 context, implies a rejection of Israel's right to territorial integrity. It sends the opposite message.

A person might say I am being unfair, that a Palestinian flag merely supports Palestinian self-determination. Sorry, no. Not in the current climate. When we have people chanting "From the river to the sea" while wrapped in keffiyehs and waving Palestinian flags, those symbols take on very particular meanings. It is disingenuous to don a keffiyeh, tack Palestinianism onto a land acknowledgement and add a Palestinian flag to your email signature and then act all innocent, as though that is not a deliberately provocative act.

The prevailing narrative of the "pro-Palestinian" movement now is intolerance. Those waving flags and wearing keffiyehs are not calling for peace and coexistence. They are calling for the destruction of Israel. This is not the path to peace. We need to hear the moderate voices, those calling for a negotiated two-state solution, and we are not hearing these voices from the "pro-Palestinian" side.

The idea that sporting keffiyehs and waving Palestinian flags, in this context, are benign symbols is akin to the contemptible reasoning that a swastika is merely an ancient Hindu symbol. Context and timing change meaning.

While these things are happening, apparently without consequences, I have heard from many people who no longer feel like they can wear a Star of David necklace in public. A school teacher told me that her teacher colleagues were stirring up anti-Jewish sentiment disguised as anti-Zionism and she felt afraid in her school's lunchroom.

I encouraged letter writers to communicate their concerns directly to their own MLAs, as well as to the Premier, and to copy me on their correspondence. My colleagues needed to see the fear that members of my community were sharing with me. I needed my colleagues to know what their constituents were experiencing, and the Premier's Office needed to see the volume of concerns.

Given the number of expressions that reached me, it is notable that not one MLA came to talk with me about the letters they were receiving from their constituents.

Not a single soul.

## *Premier urges silence*

During the first few weeks after the massacre and as Israeli troops began their response, the Premier asked caucus members to not comment on the conflict.

This may have been well-intentioned, but it missed the mark.

The rationale was that, as a subnational government, we should be concerning ourselves with the needs of British Columbians, not international conflicts. Fair enough—I had no need to comment on the conflict.

However, there is a difference between commenting on a conflict half a world away and addressing the related impacts of that conflict on British Columbians. Jewish people were being subjected to incessant messages of hatred and were fearing for their physical safety—and especially for the safety of their kids and grandkids on university and college campuses.

I was between a rock and a hard place. My people were experiencing levels of antisemitism unseen in generations and the Premier had conflated that with an overseas conflict, stifling my ability to advocate for and empathize with a community under siege—*my* community.

My task was to walk that fine line between supporting the Jewish community and not providing public commentary on the conflict between Hamas and Israel—easy to say, nearly impossible to do.

While I was forced to hold my tongue, other New Democrats increasingly felt no such obligation.

## *Sharks begin circling*

The decision to make Holocaust education mandatory in British Columbia was not a response to the events of October 7. Government doesn't work that fast.

When Premier Eby, Education Minister Rachna Singh, George Heyman and I gathered with Jewish community leaders for the announcement, on Monday, October 30, 2023, it was the culmination of a long journey.

Many British Columbians, including elected officials, were surprised to learn that Holocaust education was not already mandatory in BC. A student could graduate from high school in the province without ever hearing about this history. This is true in many provinces.

Of course, that doesn't mean students do not learn about the Holocaust. Mr. Henderson, my History 12 teacher at Richmond High, provided one of the most memorable lessons of my high school experience. I recall walking into the portable—yes, we had portables even back then—and Mr. Henderson greeted us at the door and, unlike any other day, he told us each where to sit. Some of us were sent to the front of the room, others to the back. He then went on with the lesson, which I don't think even had anything to do with the Holocaust. It wasn't the content that stayed with me all these years, it was the way he taught the class.

When he asked a question, he would praise only some students, regardless of whether they got the right answer. When he returned graded exams, he had lovely things to say to some who had barely passed and admonished others who did well. Something was amiss.

Before the class ended, Mr. Henderson engaged us in a conversation about what the previous hour had felt like. He asked what we noticed, what we were feeling and how we responded to what seemed like unfair treatment. Then he confessed that when he greeted us at the door, he sorted us based on our eye colour, with brown-eyed students being treated poorly and all others treated with privilege. This was our introduction to the lessons on the Holocaust. I remember very little by way of specific lessons from my Richmond High days, but I have never forgotten that one.

I am so grateful that Mr. Henderson chose to teach us about the Holocaust back then. I had no idea, though, until summer 2023 when Rob Fleming, the then-MLA for Victoria-Swan Lake who had earlier served as Minister of Education, told me that it was not a mandatory part of our schooling. A team in the Ministry of Education had been working to make it a required part of the curriculum.

Rob wasn't sure what had transpired after he left the portfolio—but in 2020 the pandemic hit and many things that were not emergencies got shuffled to the back burner.

After my conversation with Rob, I called the Premier's Office to ask about the progress and the Premier expressed support for making Holocaust education mandatory. He agreed with me on setting a timeline for announcing it—International Holocaust Remembrance Day, on January 27, 2024. We started getting the details in order.

After October 7, the experiences of isolation and fear in the Jewish community made me rethink our timing for announcing mandatory Holocaust education in British Columbia. The Premier's Office agreed and we advanced an earlier date for the announcement.

Teaching about the Holocaust conveys important lessons about what can happen when hate is allowed to go unchecked. At the same time, and as crucial as Holocaust education is, I do not want to suggest this is a master key to resolving antisemitism or other forms of hate and bias. There are no shortcuts in fighting racism—and antisemitism, often called "the oldest hatred," is particularly challenging for a range of reasons. An overemphasis on the Holocaust in the absence of understanding the longer history of antisemitism might lead people to think this was an aberration and therefore a thing of the past. The Holocaust, we need to remember, was part of a continuum of antisemitism that pre-existed the Nazis and that has survived them. The Holocaust was possible in scope because of the geographic reach of the Third Reich, the systematic, mechanized, assembly-line forms the killings took, and (remember Évian) the complicity of most of the world. But the hatred that caused it did not emerge in the 1930s and it did not die in 1945. Holocaust education must be taught in ways that reflect these complex realities.

It was a packed house at Vancouver's Jewish Community Centre on October 30 as Premier Eby acknowledged me and told the crowd that I was playing an important role in his caucus and cabinet ensuring the Jewish community's voices were heard. We then proceeded with a few more speeches about how this curriculum change would be a tool to advance understanding and stanch growing antisemitism.

After the announcement, Global News reporter Kristen Robinson (no relation) asked if I would do an on-camera response to recent comments by Langara College instructor Natalie Knight. Three weeks after the October 7 pogrom, Knight stood before a crowd at an anti-Israel rally at the Vancouver Art Gallery and celebrated the mass murders, rapes, immolations and kidnappings as an "amazing, brilliant offensive."

Knight had been put on administrative leave by the college, pending a review. The reporter asked me, as Minister of Post-Secondary Education, what I thought of her comments.

"I was horrified that any human being would somehow think that there was glory in what we witnessed, what Hamas perpetrated against people, against babies, old people, young people dancing in the desert," I said.

My comments were pretty tame. Honestly, I cannot believe we live in a world where anyone could find fault with what I said—or that anyone could utter the words Knight did. Surely we can agree that mass murder, rape, kidnapping, torture and burning people alive are always abhorrent.

But I guess that's the Pollyanna in me.

My statement to Global News, I believe, was when the sharks began circling. The "crappy piece of land" was the blood in the water that they got me on a few weeks later. But, from the moment I went public and condemned the celebration of rape and baby-killing as "brilliant" and "amazing," I became a target.

On social media especially, I was being singled out as an evil Zionist. Protesters would soon begin chanting my name and carrying signs at the BC NDP convention saying "Selina, Selina, you can't hide. You're committing genocide."

I was also accused of attempting to influence the Langara College administration because I was the Minister of Post-Secondary Education who expressed an opinion about a comment made by one of their instructors. In fact, the administration made their decision to put Knight on leave without any input from me.

A couple of months later, on January 23, 2024, the college reinstated Knight. The reinstatement was premised on the conclusion that her remarks were within the "bounds of protected expression." But her return was contingent on her commitment that "any future remarks could not reasonably be interpreted as celebrating violence against civilians."

I posted on social media my surprise that Knight was reinstated.

As the Minister of Post-Secondary Education, but also as the liaison to the Jewish community, I was going to have to explain the decision, so I had a meeting with the college administrators to understand their reasoning. I was not trying to influence an outcome, just listening to how they came to the decision. Knight's reinstatement was largely moot, though.

At a rally just off campus, she declared: "It means I did nothing wrong. It means none of you are doing anything wrong." She was fired on January 26.

Her union stood by her, insisting she was unfairly fired.

"Because the comment was made off of work time, it really is a freedom of expression issue," Michael Conlon, Executive Director of the Federation of Post-Secondary Educators of BC, told Global. He then called for my resignation, alleging I had a hand in her firing, which would be undue influence on a college by a political official.

Whether Knight's comments fell within her rights to free expression, and therefore did not justify her firing, is a determination a court should adjudicate. I get that a union is obligated to defend their members. But as a matter of human decency, imagine a group representing educators not only defending the right of someone to rejoice in mass murder but calling for an elected official's resignation for condemning those words. What about *my* right to free expression?

"If the minister is allowed to get away with it in this circumstance, it will put a chill on speech across the province and people will be afraid to speak out and voice their opinions," Conlon told Global News.

After Knight was dismissed, I was viciously attacked on social media again for allegedly influencing an independent decision. Social media attacks are part of a politician's job and they can be hurtful. Generally, though, they are just a drip, drip, drip of background noise. For me, that is what these attacks were. By this point, it was January 2024, and within days, social media would have a lot more to say about me.

## *Convention hoopla*

In between when Natalie Knight made her appalling remarks, in late October, and when she was fired, in January, there were almost too many small crises and major indignities to count.

The BC NDP convention was scheduled for November 17 to 19 and constituency executives were proposing multiple emergency resolutions on Gaza for debate.

I raised my concerns with the Premier's team, including Matt Smith, his Chief of Staff. I pointed out that spending time debating resolutions for which we had absolutely zero responsibility, zero expertise and zero legitimacy would not only distract us from our core issues, but would convey to the Jewish community that they cannot trust our government to deal in a balanced way with this topic at a time of massive antisemitism.

I kept coming back to the basic fact that as a provincial party we have no international responsibilities, and so it is inappropriate to have this debate. From my perspective, any international resolutions should be ruled out of order because a provincial government can't act on them. If party members have concerns on international affairs, they should take them to the federal NDP convention to be debated there. But there were apparently precedents for international resolutions at our provincial conventions. I was fighting a losing battle.

An alternative solution was recommended.

Rather than have several different constituency executives bring forward their own resolutions, we could organize ourselves to advance a single resolution that was balanced and comprehensive, that called for the release of Israeli hostages, endorsed a bilateral ceasefire, condemned the deaths of innocent civilians in Israel and Gaza, advocated for the Canadian government to provide humanitarian aid, and called for the BC government to welcome refugees from Gaza.

I could live with that.

For my mental health, I decided it was best for me to not be at the convention on the day the resolution was debated. I already had too much evidence of the tactless, insensitive and problematic behaviours of some of my elected colleagues. What individual delegates on the convention floor might say—unconstrained by the Premier's order to keep mum—was anyone's guess.

The Whip agreed and gave me leave from the convention that day. I told the Premier and Matt that it would just be too difficult for me to be in the room and to listen to people with no knowledge or connection to the place discuss Israel and its history in ways that would almost certainly telescope the message that they do not care whether people like me live or die. I may not have used those precise words, but this is how it felt to me in the moment. It is fair to say that is also how many Jewish people would have heard the debate.

While this behind-the-scenes action was taking place inside the convention hall, there was a mob of angry, hateful protesters outside calling for my head. Ostensibly, this was because I had the moral clarity to condemn Natalie Knight's words two weeks earlier. I say "ostensibly" because that is the only statement I had made that could plausibly justify their outrage. I had, of course, spoken on behalf of the government at the Jewish community vigil—so maybe they were outraged that I was grieving the mass murder of hundreds of Jewish civilians.

The only other explanation for their outrage is that I'm a Jew.

These masked and keffiyeh-covered protesters were not the sort of people who were likely to engage in a thoughtful discussion about just what it was about me that inspired such white-hot rage, so I'll leave their motivations aside.

It was notable, though, that I was the only MLA named by the protesters.

They swarmed the Victoria Conference Centre's main entrance and MLAs were advised to use alternate doors.

There was plenty of reason to fear what might happen on the floor, as we had already seen some inexcusable comments not just from anonymous individuals on social media but from leading figures on Canada's left.

Fred Hahn, the head of the Ontario branch of the Canadian Union of Public Employees and vice-president of CUPE National, glorified the massacre. On October 7, he "liked" a tweet from a CUPE local declaring: "Palestine is rising . . ."

The day after the attacks, on Thanksgiving weekend, Hahn posted on social media: "As we all think about reasons to be thankful this #thanksgiving2023, I know I'm thankful for the power of workers, the power of resistance around the globe. Because #Resistance is fruitful and no matter what some might say, #Resistance brings progress, and for that, I'm thankful." In case anyone missed his meaning, he followed it up soon after with "From the river to the sea, Palestine will be free."

Fortunately, the resolution at the BC NDP convention as presented passed and without much fuss, I am told. Still, I was exhausted and deeply saddened by the one-sided condemnation of Israel, lack of empathy for Jewish people and the unhelpful approach of this resolution. I was frustrated with the "pro-Palestinian" movement more broadly.

There is a reason I place the term "pro-Palestinian" in quote marks. The people who call themselves that rarely do Palestinian people any favours.

The only way peace will come, and the only way Palestinians will ever have national self-determination, is through a negotiated, two-state settlement. The more inflammatory and slanted the world's approach to this conflict, the further away we push compromise and therefore peace and Palestinian self-determination.

The one-sided and sometimes hysterical approach to Israel much of the left has adopted will not advance a negotiated settlement. But, as we hear from the chanting activists, negotiation is not on their agenda. Top voices on Canada's left view beheading and rape as "resistance." Their position on peace and coexistence could not be clearer. One can argue whether that is antisemitism. But it is not "pro-Palestinian." It is not "pro-peace."

It suggests to me that, for many "pro-Palestinian" activists, the goal is not peace or Palestinian self-determination. If it were, they would be chanting as much against Hamas as against the Israeli government. They would be calling for Hamas to surrender, not for Israel to give up fighting them. The goal of these activists, it seems, is just intensifying hostility toward Israel and Jews. And if that results in hundreds or thousands more dead Palestinians, it almost seems that is a price these activists are happy to pay. It sometimes appears that they revel in the number of dead innocents in Gaza.

There are terms for people like these but "pro-Palestinian" and "pro-peace" don't seem like the right ones.

## *A double standard*

When everything hit the fan, the support I received from the Jewish community and so many others was enormous and uplifting. There were, however, some less thoughtful comments.

There was a certain amount of "I told you so" from some quarters of the Jewish community. There are some Jewish people and others who believe that the left is irredeemably antisemitic and I got what was inevitably coming to me.

I did not appreciate this attitude, of course—it wasn't helpful in any way.

The bigger issue is that there should be no contradiction between being a Zionist and being a progressive.

Zionism, despite being used too often as a pejorative, is simply the movement for Jewish national self-determination. Progressives almost always support national self-determination.

Moreover, Zionism has created, in Israel, an oasis of democratic pluralism, a multicultural miracle, a place where women, ethnic and religious minorities, the LGBTQ+ community and all people are legally equal. Like any society, it is imperfect. Funding to mostly Arab communities is often not the same as funding to mostly Jewish communities. It's not that different from what other nations struggle with, whether it's differences in support and resources for rural versus urban areas or support for different cultural or linguistic communities. And yes, there is racism in Israel between Ashkenazi (typically lighter-skinned European Jews) and Sephardi or Mizrachi Jews (typically darker-skinned Arab Jews). Israel is far from perfect, but what Israelis have built in seven decades should be a model for the world. Instead, far too often, it is condemned, rather than emulated.

The fact that Israelis have achieved all this while under siege by enemies who include some of the most racist, misogynistic, homophobic, intolerant and violent terrorists and tyrants on earth should make it a natural ally to progressives. Rather than trying to eliminate Israel from the region, we should be advocating that Israeli values of democracy, multiculturalism and coexistence be spread more widely across the Middle East and North Africa. A tiny window of light has emerged with the advent of the Abraham Accords—and even this little light of hope is condemned by many on the anti-Israel side.

It is true that Israel does not have a progressive government right now. But we do not call for the elimination of the United States when we don't like their leaders. We do not mobilize a global crusade against countries with truly awful governments like China, North Korea, Iran or scores of other places.

This level of hostility is reserved for one state alone. The Jewish state.

When I see the left's obsession with Israel, I can understand where some of the "I told you so" attitude in the Jewish community comes from. However, I do not believe the left is inherently antisemitic, just as I do not believe the right is inherently antisemitic. There are antisemitic people on both sides. And regrettably, everywhere else.

However, I do have to acknowledge, after all I have been through, that there is a problem in Canada's left—in the New Democratic Party, in many of our trade unions, in the activist sector, in some social service and nongovernmental organizations, and in the LBGTQ+ community. The problem is not so much the strident clamour of the anti-Israel protesters and the sometimes antisemitic rage of the few, but the overwhelming inaction of the many in response to those few.

Jewish people, including some who have devoted our lives to building our progressive movements, have felt abandoned and betrayed by our progressive allies—by the hateful extremists but also by the silence of good people. This was true before October 7. Since then, it has become a crisis.

Some insist that it is our Zionism that makes us unwelcome, not our Jewish identity. But for me, and for the vast majority of Jewish Canadians, our Zionism is a deeply held and intrinsic part of our Jewishness.

University of Toronto sociologist Dr. Robert Brym published "Jews and Israel 2024: A Survey of Canadian Attitudes and Jewish Perceptions," in *Canadian Jewish Studies / Études juives canadiennes* spring 2024 issue. His research found that 91 percent of Canadian Jews believe Israel has a right to exist—this is the definition of a "Zionist"—with six percent answering "don't know" and three percent saying Israel does not have a right to exist. These are numbers worth keeping in mind when anti-Zionist fringe groups claim to speak for Canadian Jews. Their views represent about three in 100 Canadian Jews. Depending on the region of the country we live in, between 25 and 40 percent of Canadian Jews say they are "very" emotionally attached to Israel. When we add "somewhat" emotionally attached, the combined number among all Canadian Jews spikes to 70 percent. In other words, almost all Jews believe Israel has a right to exist and an overwhelming majority feel emotionally attached to the country.

For Jews, Israel is an intrinsic part of who we are. If that is inconvenient for some in whose ideological interest it is to separate my identities into segregated parts, that is their problem, not mine. Other people do not get to decide which components of my identity are legitimate or acceptable. They may say I am not welcome because I am a Zionist. That tells me I am unwelcome because I am a Jew.

Those who attack us because we are Zionists insist we have no right to feel attacked as Jews. It's a false dichotomy. The bigger issue is not that a small cadre of aggressive activists attack us at all—it is that the vast majority of otherwise good people stand silently while they do.

If there is one thing above all that I have taken away from this wrenching experience, it is that silence can be as painful as cruel words.

There is an axiom in the antiracist movement that there is no such thing as "not racist." There is only racist and antiracist. This is not a fence one can straddle. We are on one side or the other.

What I have learned, painfully, is that even if most people on the left do not engage in overtly antisemitic behaviours, they seem to demonstrate remarkably little concern about those who do.

I experienced a litany of offences against me and, more agonizingly, against my community by some of my colleagues on the left. But more than the acts of commission, what really hurt are the acts of omission by others. My colleagues showed up when it was uncontentious, when it cost nothing, like when Holocaust survivors visited the Legislature. Yet when there were terror supporters on the lawn of the Legislature, chanting outside my window for death to me and my people, my colleagues could not even walk down the hallway to stand by my side.

It should not be contentious to stand with the Jewish people—and against mass murder—but we have already seen that to do so is likely to brand one a Zionist like that's a bad thing and set the mob at one's heels. Still, as elected officials, we either have the courage of our convictions or we don't. And, overwhelmingly, my former colleagues did not.

To understand the power of their silence, we have to understand the opportunities they had to stand on the right side of history. One after another, a number of my colleagues in the BC NDP engaged in small and large acts of offence against Jews over the years. Every time, they were not condemned but excused. They were forgiven in every instance. There were no crowds calling for their resignation. No firings. No assignments of "deep work."

Compare this with my experience. I made an impolitic remark—and one that was not at all historically inaccurate and should not have evoked much concern at all. It was used as an excuse to end my career in cabinet. When you treat Jewish people differently than you treat anyone else, there's a word for that.

I'm not arguing that we should be less forgiving in politics. On the contrary. I am drawing attention to situations that were inarguably more problematic than anything I said but that resulted in few or no consequences for my colleagues.

On occasion, there have been inappropriate Nazi references made during an impassioned speech. These are inappropriate because they diminish the seriousness of Jewish history by abusing it for crude political advantage. These comments are often retracted, readily and quickly without much fuss, once the perpetrator realizes that their comparison diminished the impact of the Holocaust and the murder of six million Jews. Forgiveness was granted.

Jennifer Whiteside, MLA for New Westminster-Coquitlam, posted on social media back in 2014 that Israel is guilty of "pinkwashing"—a conspiracy theory in which Israel is accused of trying to deke out the world with queer rights to distract from the oppression of Palestinians. The convoluted idea that Israelis are engaged in a shell game in which one group's rights are a shiny diversion to distract the world from the abrogation of another group's rights, is an idea that is sustainable only if you carry pre-existing antisemitic ideas about devious, manipulative Jews. She was forgiven.

Ronna-Rae Leonard, who was the MLA for Courtenay-Comox, expressed public support for Arab-Israeli Haneen Zoubi, a former member of Israel's Parliament, the Knesset, who has been accused of inciting against the Israeli state and military. Zoubi views Iran as a positive force in the region and in 2010 was aboard the *MV Mavi Marmara*, part of the "Gaza Flotilla," when fatal clashes broke out with the Israeli military. One can agree or disagree with Zoubi's extremist views, but when a Canadian elected official sides with this sort of figure, Jewish Canadians can rightly question her judgment. Media covered Ronna-Rae's support for this extremist and BC Liberals called for her firing during the election, but she suffered no serious consequences.

Rachna Singh, then-MLA for Surrey Green Timbers and at the time Parliamentary Secretary for Antiracism Initiatives, set up a meeting with representatives of the Jewish community several years ago. In putting together a roundtable, she invited Independent Jewish Voices to participate. It is difficult to explain how inappropriate it was to invite this group to a talk about antisemitism. IJV is a fringe element in the Jewish community. It is safe to say, I think, it is loathed by most Jewish people who are familiar with their positions. They are seen as providing a Jewish fig leaf for the worst anti-Zionist and antisemitic voices in Canada. To make a clunky analogy, to invite IJV to a discussion on antisemitism would be akin to inviting gay "conversion" therapists to an anti-homophobia meeting. It would be like inviting anti-choice activists to a session on women's reproductive freedoms. It betrayed profound ignorance of the community. Jewish community leaders were aghast that IJV would be included in a conversation about antisemitism when they represent a tiny extremist minority. If Rachna had reached out to me, as a Jewish colleague with specific knowledge about this community, I would have been able to head off a minor disaster that hurt the Jewish community.

If a parallel affront had happened to any other ethnocultural community, the Parliamentary Secretary for Antiracism Initiatives might have been quickly shuffled out of the role. Instead, she got a pass.

On International Holocaust Remembrance Day in 2024, Premier Eby's official social media declared, "We stand with the Muslim community throughout Canada on this sorrowful day of remembrance."

It turned out, according to the retraction from the Premier, that a member of his team had accidentally posted that comment on the day for Holocaust remembrance when it was intended for two days later, on the anniversary of the 2017 shooting in a Québec City-area mosque, in which six Muslims were murdered. It was a foul-up—but a big one. Whoever was responsible for that wasn't fired. The Premier, on whose feed the statement appeared, apologized and moved on.

On May 6, 2024, Yom HaShoah, a day to commemorate those murdered in the Holocaust, there was a debate in the Legislature about the rise in antisemitism across campuses. Michael Lee, then-MLA for Vancouver-Langara, stood in the House and called on the government to use the International Holocaust Remembrance Alliance (IHRA) definition of antisemitism that had been adopted by over 40 countries, including Canada, to contest the hateful rhetoric on campuses here in British Columbia.

Michael referenced the odious comments of Charlotte Kates, a local activist and head of Samidoun Palestinian Prisoner Solidarity Network, which the federal government soon after designated a terrorist entity. Michael outlined some of the attacks on Jewish students, hateful protests at the Jewish campus centre Hillel, and the fruitless calls made to the president of the University of British Columbia to take action.

Up again popped Aman Singh, the first of my colleagues after October 7 to set off alarms for me by ignoring the Israeli dead and demanding that we announce our solidarity with Palestinians.

This time, Aman responded in the House by repeatedly referencing a letter signed by a fringe group of anti-Israel Jewish faculty. Aman chose to quibble over the definition of antisemitism, rather than confront anti-Jewish racism. Instead of standing with a besieged community and with Jewish students on campus, he chose to defend the rising harassment, fear and intimidation that Jewish students, faculty and staff were experiencing on the grounds of free expression. This is something we have seen repeatedly as we try to address the antisemitism epidemic: People who in any other case, with any other group of people but Jews, would be racing to the side of the targeted community, obscure the issue with equivocations around definitions, hedging over whether a violent attack was motivated by racism or mere politics, doing everything except what antiracist, progressive people should do in a situation like this.

Aman highlighted a single letter from a marginal, unrepresentative group while ignoring the letters his own Jewish constituents were sending him, the plentiful evidence of police reports, and the fact that Charlotte Kates was under arrest and being investigated for possible contravention of Canada's hate speech laws. He couldn't bring himself to condemn the incontrovertible anti-Jewish racism we were seeing without nit-picking over whether it fit this or that definition.

Most disgracefully, he chose to do this on a day when Holocaust survivors were in the legislative building to mourn those murdered in the Holocaust.

The government no doubt heard from outraged community members and, I'm sure ordered by the Premier's Office, Aman stood in the House the next day and apologized.

"I would like to take a moment to clarify some comments I made yesterday morning," he said. "I made remarks about how government must be circumspect in policing speech, but it's also important to say that a protest can never be a shield for antisemitism or, indeed, any form of hate. We must defend free speech while also calling out hate, and I missed that balance yesterday. It's a delicate balance.

"In my speech, I did indirectly reference the arrest of Charlotte Kates for her comments on October 7 as an example that our system indeed works. Her comments may have amounted to hate speech, and she was arrested for that. But upon reflection, I wish I had taken more time to name and recognize the harm of comments like hers and explicitly call out the antisemitism and hate that we have seen at several protests.

"I'm genuinely sorry for not doing that, especially on Yom HaShoah.

"Yesterday was a day to remember Holocaust victims and to redouble our commitments to fighting antisemitism. I know this is an extremely difficult time for the Jewish community, especially on campuses. I understand that on a very personal level, especially as a visually identifiable Sikh, part of a community that has also been historically targeted and marginalized.

"I'm an ardent believer in teachable moments and I look forward to meeting with members of the Jewish community and to continuing to dialogue and learn how to be an effective ally in fighting antisemitism and hate."

I didn't buy it for a minute. I had seen Aman's "apologies" before.

Six months earlier when the Premier ordered Aman to apologize to me for his insensitivity in the days after the massacre, Aman sent me a perfunctory message that was an explanation, not an apology. He seemed to have learned nothing from his earlier disastrous foray into this topic. He still seemed to believe that calling for the destruction of Israel and the annihilation of Jews was mere freedom of expression. Not exactly the words of an ally in fighting antisemitism.

And the pattern continues.

A progressive government that says it values minority groups and stands up to racism finds itself having to apologize again and again to the Jewish community as its members engage in deplorable commentary that justifies antisemitism and violence.

There were no other consequences for Aman. No antisemitism training. No requirement to step down from responsibilities. No "deep work" of any sort. Just an apology and a commitment to meet with members of the Jewish community.

The point is not that these incidents should have ended in a flurry of firings. The point is that everyone gets forgiven for impolitic remarks, bad choices and grievous mistakes.

Everyone except the Jew.

When I made a remark that a few agitated activists took exception to, all hell broke loose. I was fired, received death threats and became persona non grata. Again: There's a word for that.

Other colleagues have disappointed in other ways, which I detailed at some length in my resignation letter from the New Democrat caucus, which is reprinted later.

But then there is Mable Elmore, MLA for Vancouver-Kensington. This case is worth delving into a bit because it reflects a double standard that makes even the litany of previous bad judgments and inappropriate remarks pale.

When she was an organizer for the bus drivers' union, Mable told an interviewer in *Seven Oaks* magazine that "we have vocal Zionists in our work sites, and we've had to battle them."

I had heard of "Zionist bankers," "Zionist puppet-masters" and all sorts of supposed Zionist plots before, but Zionist bus drivers was a fresh one even for a Jew with my not insignificant familiarity with kooky conspiracies. She got a free pass despite this bizarre statement.

From her earliest days in politics, obviously, Mable has not been a person with whom the Jewish community felt safe to engage—she is not trusted, and she has never apologized for her hurtful comments. But what did David Eby do as soon as he became Premier? He put her in charge of antiracism initiatives.

The Jewish community was stunned.

How could the Premier put Mable Elmore, of all people, in charge of the antiracism file when she has had such a troubled history with the Jewish community? As the Jew in the Crew, I went out on a limb. I brokered space and opportunity for the Jewish community to give Mable a chance. The community knew me and, at my urging, gave Mable the benefit of the doubt.

I was wrong. That was the eternal optimist in me, hoping that people would change.

Indeed, Mable showed up on October 10, 2023, at the Jewish community's vigil for those murdered and kidnapped by Hamas, which surprised many of us. But if this was a sign she was turning over a new leaf, the next month she destroyed what little trust she may have built.

In November 2023, Mable delivered a statement in the Legislature ostensibly marking Transgender Day of Remembrance. She quickly veered into the Hamas-Israel conflict, omitting the fact that Hamas started the war by murdering almost 1,200 people and kidnapping 250 others. She completely ignored the horrors of October 7, as though they had never happened. Her biased, morally obscene statement was bad enough in content. In context, it was even more inappropriate. She hid her decision to speak on the subject from the Whip and the entire caucus, blindsiding all of us and explicitly contravening the Premier's directive to stay silent on the subject.

I knew that the Jewish community would be outraged, as I was, that the Parliamentary Secretary for Antiracism Initiatives would choose to purvey a one-sided narrative that blamed Israel for a conflict that was initiated by Hamas.

I went to the Premier's Chief of Staff, Matt Smith, and let him know my concerns and the impact Mable's choice had on the Jewish community. I told Matt that Mable's speech felt like a "Fuck you to me and to the Jewish community writ large." Her actions were grounds to remove her from the file. Mable knew that her statement would not be approved by the Whip's office—so she misled the leadership. This was not poor judgment. She made a choice. I wanted to know how this behaviour could be acceptable to the Premier. Matt listened and said he would consider what I was saying.

Shortly afterward, the Premier told the leadership in the Jewish community that their engagement with the antiracism file would now be handled directly by Niki Sharma, the Attorney General, who has overall responsibility for antiracism initiatives.

Singling out the Jewish community because the Parliamentary Secretary for Antiracism Initiatives insulted our community—one of the communities she is supposed to be serving in her antiracism role and inarguably one of those facing the most urgent crisis—was inexcusable. Instead of addressing Mable's problem, the Premier did a workaround to exclude the Jewish community, as though it was our behaviour that led to this problem, not Mable's. I cannot imagine this issue being mismanaged more completely.

With Mable now responsible for antiracism initiatives affecting *every ethnocultural group except Jews*, responsibility for addressing antisemitism moved up the chain to the Attorney General.

By January 2024, weeks had passed since Mable had been stripped of her responsibility to combat antisemitism, and things were only getting worse for Jews on our campuses and in our streets. I contacted Niki to see what progress was being made.

I asked what she was hearing from the Jewish community and what her office was doing given the sustained rise in antisemitism. We were three months post-October 7 and the Premier had met once with a handful of Jewish leaders—aside from regular contact with me, no other formal outreach had occurred from our government.

Niki had received responsibility for engaging with the Jewish community early in December—six weeks before I reached out to her. When I asked if she had met with any community leaders or organizations yet, she responded, "Oh right. I should follow up on that."

I reminded her—I should not have had to—that this is a community under siege. I asked her what she and her team were thinking in terms of supporting a community that is dealing with a level of hatred unseen in generations. She responded with a boilerplate of previously announced public initiatives and political bafflegab.

I pushed her to acknowledge that none of those things would make people safer or address rising antisemitism. I did my best to keep my frustration in check as I challenged her for responding to me as if I were an opposition member or a voter, rather than a colleague whose own community is reeling from racist hatred.

She did offer me one thing—a briefing about upcoming anti-racism legislation and other initiatives around racism. I said sure, I would welcome a briefing.

It never happened.

The disappointments became increasingly personal.

In December 2023, the Coquitlam Teachers Association issued an anti-Israel diatribe, which they took the trouble to send to me and other MLAs, even though it was addressed to the Prime Minister. It was as though they didn't understand the difference between orders of government. Apparently assuming that Justin Trudeau was lying awake at night wondering what the Coquitlam Teachers Association thought about Israel and Palestine, the letter was an unhinged harangue replete with all the slogans and rhetoric you would expect from a social media diatribe, not from professionals we entrust to teach our next generations.

I was friends with Ken Christensen, the head of the teachers' union local, who signed the letter. When teachers went on strike because of the Christy Clark government's intransigence, I was on the picket lines with them. I stood with Ken against the activists who were opposing the government's sexual orientation and gender identity (SOGI) initiatives. I was right by his side as an ally and as a parent of a gay son, pushing back on hate against queer people. And now he was spreading hate against my people.

I got a phone call from a Jewish parent who had seen the letter on the CTA's website and was going to pull their kids out of the public school system. I am a strong believer in public schools, but when Jewish kids don't feel safe there and parents are thinking about pulling them out, we have a big problem.

I asked Ken for a meeting and I had his letter in front of me. I called him on his claims. I barraged him with questions.

*What is apartheid and how does that term apply here?* I asked him. *What is ethnic cleansing and when has that happened in Palestine? How did you decide that Jews are not indigenous, but Palestinians are? Where did Jews come from? What's the history of Palestine? When was Palestine a nation-state? What happened in 1948 that resulted in Israel becoming a state? Where are you getting your evidence? Where are your voices around Chad, Ukraine, Uighurs, Syria, Sudan, Yemen, Ethiopia, Congo? How do you think this perspective affects Jewish children in our community?*

He had no answers. He knew nothing. He's a teacher whose intervention on this subject demonstrated profound ignorance, which is bad enough. But he also signed the letter, which was filled with hyperbole, innuendo and rhetoric that he could not justify or explain. He told me it was really his executive that wanted to send the letter.

This is a phenomenon that is incredibly common on this topic. After October 7, many individuals and organizations lent their names and credibility to letters or petitions that were inflammatory and biased. Again and again, when challenged, they would back off. They would admit they didn't know what they were signing, plead ignorance, acknowledge they're not an expert and so they misunderstood the issues, say they didn't think it would be controversial, claim they hadn't really read it. They would recant or otherwise distance themselves from what they had done.

This was precisely what Ken did.

Even if race-hatred were not at the root of this behaviour, how could this sort of hyperbolic, one-sided, ill-informed, unresearched campaign be acceptable coming from a group representing educators? If a student handed in something like this, they would deserve an F.

Is this how we teach peace? Unions know that the best agreement is hammered out at the negotiating table. I asked Ken why they weren't calling for Palestinians and Israelis to come to the table. Where is the union's commitment to negotiation in this instance? Absent. Instead of advancing a negotiated settlement that could lead to peace, the anti-Israel movement demonizes Israel, which pushes peace and Palestinian self-determination further away. By polarizing the parties, they ensure continued conflict and death, even while self-righteously wrapping themselves in the language of peace and coexistence.

But it wasn't Ken who upset me most around this incident. This was yet another instance of a small group driving incendiary division and those who should call it out remaining silent.

I asked Fin Donnelly, my caucus colleague from Coquitlam-Burke Mountain, if he got the same letter. He had. I asked what he was going to do about it. He told me he was going to ignore it.

Is this leadership? Is that what we should expect from our elected representatives if a group as important in our community as the association that represents teachers posted on their website and widely disseminated a prejudiced, hateful diatribe against any other ethnic or national group?

Imagine a trade union, a teachers' union no less, posting a letter on their website undermining the right to self-determination of any other nation. That would be bad enough. But imagine them doing so while that group of people is experiencing unprecedented racism right here in Canada. We should be promoting social harmony at home and compromise and coexistence worldwide, not amplifying the most polarizing, intolerant, uncompromising voices. Teachers, of all people, should know this. And if they don't, then progressive leaders in government should be the first to tell them.

Sadly, I had a remarkably similar interaction with NDP MP Bonita Zarrillo, Member of Parliament for Port Moody-Coquitlam.

Near the end of 2023, her colleague Don Davies, the NDP MP for Vancouver Kingsway, went on a weird Twitter bender about Israel, accusing it of "using sophisticated technology to target and kill leading Gazan academics, authors, historians, poets, artists, journalists, teachers . . . This is cultural genocide."

This was completely made-up. It was a "Jewish space laser"-level antisemitic conspiracy theory that can be found on the darkweb, and to see it on the social media feed of a Canadian Member of Parliament is deeply worrying.

I reached out to Bonita, as a friend and as my MP, and I said, "You need to tell Don to stop. He's looking crazy."

My experience is, when federal New Democrats look crazy, I look crazy. Rants like this taint us all.

Her response to me was, "Why don't you call him yourself?"

I said, "Because you are my MP and he's your colleague."

The least I should have been able to expect was something like, "Selina, I'm on it." Instead, she offered no help.

I am a Jewish constituent, a personal friend, a colleague who spoke at her nomination meeting and who volunteered on her campaign. And she would not even advocate for me with her own colleague who was spreading antisemitic conspiracies. This was not merely about me. It was not even about the Jewish community exclusively. This was about an MP tweeting garbage that makes our party collectively look like fringe lunatics. Yet, when I reached out to Bonita for the most minimal support, I got nothing.

Allyship is not telling someone to fight their own battles.

## *Ever thus*

Jews were deeply engaged in building the NDP, and its predecessor, the Cooperative Commonwealth Federation, as well as the union movement and much of the greater left. Without Jewish activism, from the 1930s to today, the progressive movement would probably be a shadow of itself.

Like much of the left, the NDP was overwhelmingly pro-Israel in the decades after 1948. After the Six Day War in 1967, a fundamental shift took place in the global perceptions of the conflict. This was especially pronounced on the left.

That war inverted the David-and-Goliath narrative of the Middle East. During and after 1948, Israel was the underdog defending itself against the entire Arab world. In 1967, when the Arab world again set upon Israel in an expressed war of annihilation, little David Israel won decisively—and was recast as Goliath.

Overnight, the prevailing narrative went from the entire Arab world targeting tiny Israel into a narrative of big bad Israel targeting the tiny Palestinians.

I'll acknowledge that Israel is the predominant military force in the region. If it were not, it would already have been annihilated. The refusal of its neighbours to live in peace forced Israel to become a military power—and then their neighbours (and overseas activists) condemn Israel for that. It's a no-win—though the alternatives, as Golda Meir, Israel's Prime Minister from 1969 to 1974 said, are clear: "If we have to have a choice between being dead and pitied, and being alive with a bad image, we'd rather be alive and have the bad image."

Many Jews interpret the criticism of Israel as a very clear statement that the world would rather see us as dead victims than living people capable of defending ourselves.

While the left worldwide was becoming more "pro-Palestinian" and more anti-Israel, the NDP in some ways reflected these trends more intensely than leftist parties in some other countries.

Svend Robinson (no relation) almost singlehandedly turned the federal NDP into a party that most Jews have difficulty trusting.

Robinson, NDP MP for Burnaby (riding boundaries and names changed over his career) from 1979 to 2004, was a hero to many of us as the first gay MP to come out. It was tectonic. Many of my queer friends point to that as a turning point in this country, an unprecedented change in visibility.

Robinson was also a leader on a raft of issues and he had an unparalleled knack for getting publicity. Someone once said the most dangerous place in Ottawa is between Svend Robinson and a TV camera. But he managed to shine a spotlight on so many topics, giving them attention that an opposition MP can usually only dream of.

Robinson became Parliament's most vocal "pro-Palestinian" advocate and helped turn the party away from a balanced position. He certainly laid waste to any vestiges of the NDP as a pro-Israel party.

Over the decades though, NDP leaders tried to keep a lid on this incendiary topic, mostly by avoiding the subject wherever possible.

Eventually, new leaders, first Jack Layton and then Tom Mulcair, managed to wrangle the party's credibility back by sidelining some of the extremists who had seized control of the foreign policy agenda.

This is not only strategically sound but ideologically sensible. The anti-Israel movement is fundamentally anti-progressive. The movement and its activists align with the most intolerant and violent leaders against the one oasis of liberal democracy in the region, the country with equal rights for women and every minority community. Palestinianism—either in the form of the "moderate" Fatah of the Palestinian Authority or the Hamas extremists of the Gaza Strip—doesn't demonstrate any commitment to the values we cherish. On issues affecting women, queer people and religious minorities, and on basic rights like free expression, separation of religion and state, and free collective bargaining, the current Palestinian leaders and the movement aligned with them do not even pretend to share our progressive values. The only explanation for the unity between Western progressives and Palestinian leaders is the political adage that the enemy of my enemy is my friend.

And the enemy here is Jews.

Palestinian leaders and the larger Arab body politic rarely make the polite distinctions Western activists do between "Zionists" and "Jews."

But let's say it is not overt Jew-hatred at play here.

Only through the imposition of a simplistic and distorted binary of underdog and oppressor—and a completely false narrative of colonialism and indigeneity—could progressives align with a movement that so betrays our core values. But this is what has happened.

Everything that Jack Layton and Tom Mulcair did to try to yank the party back from this extremist abyss has been undone. To me, the reversal was clear at the federal NDP convention in 2021. Then, in a 2022 letter, federal NDP leader Jagmeet Singh slammed the door on any pretense of balance or fairmindedness.

My policy interests are more local and provincial than they are federal. But I couldn't be silent when I saw some of the resolutions on the agenda of the 2021 federal convention. Of 48 resolutions under the heading "Redefining Canada's Place in the World," six resolutions singled out Israel—and these were the resolutions that were prioritized for debate.

I called my friend who I had always considered to be wise and thoughtful, Tania Jarzebiak—the campaign manager in my first run for the Legislature. Tania had spent years on the federal NDP executive. I let her know my concerns about the fixation the federal NDP has with Israel and that this was a bad look for the party. I explained that one or two resolutions would be sufficient to express concerns about Israeli government policies, but six prioritized for debate with such precious little time on the convention floor was overkill. Her response stunned me.

"It has been ever thus," she said.

That's it. In those five words she told me all I needed to know. The federal NDP has long been obsessed with Israel. They have such disdain for the sole Jewish state that they will single it out and devote lots of scheduled debate time to Israel rather than consider what is happening in China, Syria, Russia, Iran or North Korea.

It is bad enough that New Democrats have adopted a massively distorted narrative that places all the blame for this conflict on Israel alone, with no responsibility ascribed to the Palestinian terrorists or the larger decades-long Arab strategy of rejectionism. It is bad enough that some, or most, of the people behind these resolutions want to eliminate Israel as a state. It is bad enough that these resolutions directly target Israel's military advantage—a military advantage without which the people of Israel would have likely been wiped out in any of several successive Arab-initiated wars. All of this would be bad enough. But the number of resolutions, not only submitted but prioritized for debate in a necessarily limited timeframe, cannot be seen as anything other than an irrational fixation on this one country. The country of Jews.

The argument is always that Israel is just that evil, that the treatment of Palestinians is just so extraordinarily unjust, that it validates this level of attention.

Anyone with knowledge of the injustice and tragedy in the world today can see this for what it is. Even with the horrific death tolls in the current Israel-Hamas war, still the numbers of dead precisely next door, in Syria's civil war, are more than 10 to 15 times greater. This is a grotesque accounting of human lives and it horrifies me to make this case. But when 600,000 Syrians are dead and activists cannot muster so much as a candlelight vigil while a fraction of that number of people have been tragically killed in the current Israel-Hamas war and throngs march in the streets from Pretoria to Prague, there is only one explanation. How difficult is this to understand?

What is the variable here that makes this conflict eclipse others that are exponentially greater in catastrophic human impacts?

Jews.

We can doll up the details. We can find all sorts of excuses why the United Nations General Assembly devotes massively disproportionate time to condemning Israel—more condemnatory resolutions than it devotes to every other country on earth *combined*. We can justify an obsession with Israel that allows despots and genocides to go almost entirely ignored. There are always excuses. But that's what they are. Because who is going to admit the real reason that the entire world—street activists, campus campers, trade union plenaries, NDP motions, tens of thousands of people marching around the world—is concerned about the actions of this one country while ignoring injustices everywhere else?

And yet, none of these obvious warning signs of moral and ideological peril seem to have any impact on today's federal New Democrats.

In August 2022, Jagmeet Singh sent an email to a number of party members that served as a fundamental shift in approach. For whatever strategic or ideological reasons, he simply gave up any pretext of balance.

As "pro-Palestinian" activists tend to do, he couched his words in the language of "peace," "human rights" and "international law." But the radical positions expressed in the letter, which was effectively the sort of handbill you might be handed at an anti-Israel rally from a guy wrapped in a keffiyeh, serve only to advance continued conflict, intolerance and injustice.

In his letter, Singh wrote: "We believe Israel's illegal occupation of the Palestinian territories is at the centre of the challenges facing the Palestinian and Israeli people. There will be no long-term solution to the protracted conflict until the 55-year occupation ends. We condemn all violence against Israeli and Palestinian civilians, including acts of terror, as well as all acts of provocation, incitement, and destruction. We all want to see a future where Israelis and Palestinians can live side by side, in peace."

Israel had not been in Gaza from 2005 until Hamas started the current war. The occupation of Gaza ended almost two decades ago. It turned out the end of the occupation wasn't the "long-term solution to the protracted conflict" Singh thinks it is.

He hasn't learned recent history.

Singh puts the cart of ending the occupation before the horse of peace and coexistence. This is what Singh and the federal party get exactly wrong. If we want Israel to get out of Gaza and the parts of the West Bank where it still controls territory, Palestinians and their leaders need to demonstrate they are willing to live next to Israel, not instead of it, to build a country alongside Israelis, not on their graves. When Palestinian leaders decide to live in peace, there can be peace. Singh and so many others fail to recognize this prerequisite.

We also need Israeli leaders who are committed to peace, and by isolating and vilifying Israel and its people, we make this less likely because it entrenches a defensive mentality among Israeli voters and leaders.

Nevertheless, Singh's letter then goes on to make a laundry list of demands on Israel, calling for this concession and that acknowledgement, to do this and not do that. What he never does is acknowledge the root of the conflict—the Palestinian leadership's stubborn determination to use violence to end Israel's existence—and so he rewards that violence, demonizes Israel, makes coexistence less possible and makes a "free Palestine" less likely.

The narrative the federal NDP has adopted is that Israel is preventing a two-state solution and therefore anti-Israel violence is justified (or, at a minimum, understandable).

Israelis have always wanted peace and they were prepared to support a two-state solution when there seemed to be a path to get there, as there was during the Oslo Process. They will not, however, permit an independent Palestine if it will be a staging area for a succession of October 7s.

We need to acknowledge the real reason Palestine is not independent. Again and again, it has been the Palestinian leadership and the larger Arab world that have prevented a two-state solution. They have done this repeatedly.

They rejected the Partition Resolution of 1947.

They launched a war of annihilation in 1948 rather than accept coexistence.

Having failed to dislodge the Jews in 1948, they prepared for another war of annihilation in 1967. Again, they failed in their explicit goal of driving the Jews into the sea.

Immediately after that 1967 war, when Israel offered to return the Gaza Strip and the West Bank, the Arab world said no—not once but three times. At the Khartoum Conference in September 1967, the Arab leaders famously brushed aside Israel's offer to return the occupied territories in exchange for nothing but recognition and an agreement to live in peace. The Arab leaders responded with their three no's: No peace with Israel. No recognition of Israel. No negotiations with Israel. That obstinacy has sentenced Palestinians to almost six more decades of statelessness so far. But it is not only the Palestinians Arab "friends" who have undermined their interests. It has been, again and again, the Palestinians' own leaders.

When the Palestinians were closer to self-determination than ever, in 2000, they put an end to the Oslo Process and launched the Second Intifada, beginning a new phase of the conflict that continues today.

The reason for this conflict—and the reason for Palestinian statelessness—has always been, and remains, the refusal by the Palestinian leadership and the larger Arab world to coexist and to accept the basic reality of Israel's right to exist.

We can insist that Israel is preventing an independent Palestine, that Israel is the root of all evil. But the definition of insanity is doing the same thing repeatedly expecting a different result. Leftists have been blaming Israel for the impasse for at least 50 years. And peace and Palestinian self-determination have only become more remote. We can keep doing what we're doing, but it is not getting us where we claim we want to be.

It seems that Israelis and Palestinians, for many of these activists, are not real people. They are avatars in an ideological worldview. We can see this in the way self-declared "pro-Palestinian" activists tally the rising numbers of Palestinians killed in every conflict with a truly macabre relish. They wave these numbers like flags, declaring moral victory because their side has the greatest number of dead. It looks, from my vantage, that a lot of so-called "pro-Palestinian" activists would fight for Palestine to the last dead Palestinian.

Let us not forget, also, that Jews have always been an avatar, of sorts. When societies have faced difficulties, unwelcome change, uncertainty, unanswerable questions or other perplexing challenges, people have, century after century, projected their anxieties and anger onto a Jewish scapegoat. Societies in Europe, North Africa, the Middle East and elsewhere have repeatedly accused Jews of being at the root of all evil—whatever the particular evil of the moment happens to be.

Today, Canadians are faced with perplexing challenges around race, indigeneity and reconciliation, the legacies of imperialism and other forms of injustice, as well as economic inequality. How surprising is it that the empty vessel upon which they project all their messy guilt and theorizing about race, privilege, inequality and the rest of the difficult things we are struggling to deal with is Israel, *the Jewish state*?

It is not entirely this simple, of course. Many on the left view Western civilization as stained by racism, settler colonialism, oppression, and other sins that are certainly deserving of redress. Even though Israel does not come close to epitomizing these traits, it is nevertheless the Jewish state that the world has chosen to crucify as the embodiment of these evils.

When Israel is portrayed as the textbook illustration of these sins, it is not only inaccurate but is yet another projection of our own sins upon a Jewish scapegoat.

The idea that progressives, those Canadians supposedly most attuned to issues of racism, could possibly be re-enacting the prejudice of their ancestors in their approach to Jews may cause one to immediately go to denial or indignation. But what happened to the idea of listening to those with lived experience? Jews in Canada, in this moment, are living through a terrifying experience and it is progressive voices that are doing the terrifying. As progressives, we commit to listening to those with lived experience. When we are accused of racism or any other form of harm to a group of people, we pause, we consider, we reflect, we ask questions, we listen, we engage, we "do the work."

At least, that's what we do with other minority groups. But that's not what is happening when dealing with Jews.

Someone has to say it.

The left's obsession with this conflict has little or nothing to do with our feelings for Palestinians. It has everything to do with our feelings for Jews.

## *Federal* NDP *betrays progressive values*

All of this presupposes that Canadian activists are having an impact—positive or negative, depending on one's view—on events in the Middle East. I'll leave this aside for a moment and focus on the impacts of these activists here at home.

In March 2024, the federal NDP's Foreign Affairs Critic Heather McPherson led what must be one of the most acrimonious, damaging attacks on our multicultural harmony a Canadian political party has ever perpetrated.

McPherson put forward a motion to recognize Palestinian statehood, suspend the sale of military equipment to Israel and generally declare Israel bad/Palestine good. The content of the motion, eventually watered down by more than a dozen amendments, matters little. It was a non-binding motion and neither

Israelis nor Palestinians probably care much what Canada's Parliament has to say about their situation.

The motion had zero practical impact on the conflict in the Middle East. What it did was exacerbate the conflict among Canadians.

It was five months after October 7, five months since the beginning of this horrific, bloody war—and the federal NDP caucus in Parliament used this heartrending conflict for crass political advantage.

McPherson, Jagmeet Singh and the rest of the federal NDP caucus looked at Canadian multicultural communities in pain and decided to try to score some points off them.

The situation is that the federal NDP caucus was unified on one side of this issue. The federal Conservatives were unified on the other. The Liberal government and caucus were deeply divided. And so the NDP thought it would be fun to watch the Liberals squirm.

The NDP knew that one of those two communities would feel isolated and betrayed in the end, no matter how the final vote fell. And they decided that was a trade-off they were prepared to make.

The Jewish community and the Palestinian community were both used as political bludgeons in a partisan scheme.

What the NDP had done was take an issue that was explosive and agonizing for at least two cultural communities in our country and pour salt all over it. They ensured that people—no matter which side they were on—became more entrenched and divided on an already deeply painful issue.

This behaviour, this exploitation of cultural division for political gain, is so counterintuitive to everything we claim to believe as progressive people, what can justify it? When it comes to the issue of Israel and Palestine, our core progressive values too often go out the window.

In the process, we betray everything we claim to support. LGBTQ+ people are aligning with some of the most homophobic leaders and political movements on earth. Feminists are aligning with some of the most misogynistic. Human rights activists are making common cause with the most repressive entities on the planet. What is the overstrike key that allows us to do this? What is going on?

Do I really need to name it?

I have often wondered what benefit the federal party sees in poking sticks around this particular conflict. If it were a genuine concern for Palestinian well-being, as I have said, the NDP would not be promoting a polarizing, one-sided narrative. They would be encouraging dialogue and coexistence.

I assumed it must be an ideological motivation driving this, a simplistic and misleading idea that powerful Israel is oppressing powerless Palestinians. But another possibility exists, and McPherson's disappointing motion convinced me this is the likeliest explanation.

The Canadian Jewish community is small—and, as a proportion of the population, shrinking. Moreover, as the community has gone from being a mostly immigrant group to a more established ethnocultural group over the decades, many Jews have shifted right economically and politically. (Aided, of course, by NDP policies that make us feel unwelcome in the party.)

According to the census, the Canadian Muslim community is now about five times the size of the Jewish community—and growing fast. New Democrats can read those tea leaves. Voting numbers matter.

The federal NDP, I think, has made a cynical political calculation. It may be the same calculation Premier Eby made when confronted by imams and Muslim organizations threatening his party's access to Muslim voters unless I was fired.

Many Muslims are, according to opinion polls, deeply invested in the Palestinian cause. But there is a problem. Like evangelical Christians, many religious Muslims are staunchly conservative on social issues.

We have already seen a sort of unholy alliance over Palestine between parts of the left and Muslim activists who may disagree on almost every social issue, but they can find common cause on Palestine. Federal New Democrats, I think, saw that magic formula at work in the anti-Israel movement on campus, in trade unions and elsewhere, and decided to try it out for themselves.

There are liberal Muslims, to be clear, just as there are liberal Christians and liberal Jews and liberal members of every other group. But many of the people the NDP is attracting by waving the Palestinian flag high are not progressives. They may create a schism in the party that could blow the entire enterprise wide open. They may come for the Palestinianism, but they'll also stay for the debate on queer rights, reproductive freedom, women's roles in society and funding for religious educational institutions.

A few short years ago, I thought my party might be able to handle that debate. Now, I have every reason to believe that political expediency will trump basic values. The NDP has already demonstrated no loyalty to the thousands of Jews who invested decades of commitment to build the left in Canada. The NDP's commitment to fighting antisemitism is limited to hollow words—if that. Can we trust the party to be any more loyal to the things we consider inviolable to the left today? If the party becomes addicted to the votes of religious conservatives who hate Israel, what else will they sacrifice to keep those voters and activists happy? Gay rights? Feminism? Inclusive curricula? Separation of religion and state?

It sounds ludicrous, I know.

But if you had told me a few years ago that Jews would not feel welcome in the NDP, I would have called that outrageous too.

## *What I Learned at Summer Camp*

IN 2020, WHEN I was appointed by John Horgan to be Minister of Finance, I received a message from Leah Levi, the head of Camp Miriam, the Jewish summer camp where I spent several years as a counsellor.

"Make good decisions with the *kupa*," she wrote.

*Kupa* is the Hebrew term for the collective pot of money on a kibbutz, a traditionally agricultural Israeli work and living collective. Kibbutz members jointly decide whether and how to spend its revenues—and since Camp Miriam is founded on the kibbutz model, it is something I was familiar with from my days as a camp counsellor.

Her message was simple, funny—and amazingly profound. It only dawned on me then that my summer camp experiences, which had been so formative in reconnecting me with my Jewish identity as a young adult, had also provided my earliest and most crucial lessons in leadership.

To understand what happened to me as part of BC's NDP government—and by extrapolation to understand how a great many Jews in Canada and around the world have felt since October 7, 2023—it will help to know who I am and how I became this way.

I like to think I'm pretty much an open book. But politicians are inevitably perceived through a gauze of public assumptions. It may seem dramatic to suggest that this book aims to "humanize" Jewish people through the experience of a single Jewish person, but dehumanization—the tendency to see people not as individuals but as archetypes of a group or otherwise as something less than fully actualized humans—is central to antisemitism.

As much as this is my story, it is a story of a larger phenomenon. It is about how perceptions of Jews—our presumed characteristics, the assumptions others hold of us, the exceptional way the one Jewish country in the world is treated among the family of nations—influence how people treat Jews. That is what I hope readers will focus on.

Brené Brown said, "People are hard to hate close up." It is easier to dehumanize and hate people when we don't know them. Antisemitism has always presented a particular problem because it flourishes most where Jews are absent. Across centuries and continents, this absence has allowed people to project fears, hatred, discontent and misperceptions onto an empty vessel.

By the time my generation came along, though, antisemitism in Canada was mostly seen as a relic of another time and place.

For the generations of Jews after the Second World War, Canada, the United States, Australia and a few other places were, for all intents, our Promised Land. Antisemitism that had plagued our ancestors was mostly non-existent or fast declining.

Israel, which was reborn as an independent nation just three years after the end of the Holocaust, was viewed as a refuge for Jews from less fortunate parts of the world—from Europe, obviously, the surviving remnants of the Holocaust. But Israel would also be a refuge for Jews from across the Middle East and North Africa, from which close to a million Jews would be ethnically cleansed in the second half of the 20th century. Later, a million Jews from the former Soviet Union would flood into Israel. Jews from Ethiopia and other places where life was overwhelmingly hard also came. For Jews in North America, though, in the eyes of my parents' generation, we were where we belonged.

It was this idyllic, possibly naïve, comfort that made the re-emergence of antisemitism so jolting to our parents and to my own generation, who had overwhelmingly dismissed the warnings of our grandparents' generation about the potential for things to turn on a dime.

Many Jewish Canadians are descended from survivors of the Holocaust. My family fled Europe earlier. Even so, the stories of Jews' precariousness in non-Jewish societies were handed down to me.

Two of my grandparents—both my grandmothers—were born in Canada. While the Jewish community in Canada goes back to the earliest days of New France, almost all Jews in Canada descend from immigrants who arrived in the decades around the turn of the 20th century or even more recently, in the postwar period. As a third-generation Canadian Jew on both sides, I'm not exactly in the Mayflower category (or the Canadian equivalent), but mine are comparatively deep Canadian roots.

My parents grew up poor in the Montréal Jewish milieu—you might shorthand the novels of Mordecai Richler if it helps—and then, after they married, like a lot of second- and third-generation children of immigrants, my parents decamped to the suburbs to raise their kids.

In Chomedey, north of Montréal, my younger sister Stacey and younger brother Erle and I lived a pretty ideal existence. We lived in a predominantly Jewish area of town where most of the children and teachers in my public elementary were Jewish. We ran around the neighbourhood without any concerns, went to ski school in winter and Jewish summer camp.

We attended synagogue on holidays at Young Israel of Chomedey, a Modern Orthodox congregation. I was also sent to Hebrew school, the sole purpose being to learn to read the *siddur*, the prayer book. You memorized the *aleph-bet*, the Hebrew alphabet, so that you could read the prayers. It certainly wasn't my favourite after-school activity.

My father, Irv, started off working in the clothing industry, the *shmata* business, as Jews call it, the rag trade, a very typical Montréal Jewish activity. Later, he sold life insurance—he's a good salesman, so the product wasn't as important as his ability to move product.

My mom Rhoda was a stay-at-home parent, as most of our mothers were in that time and place.

Eventually, when Anglos began (rightly or wrongly) to doubt their future in Québec in the aftermath of the 1976 separatist Parti Québecois election victory, Dad bought a business in BC. When I was 14, we moved from Chomedey, where I existed in an almost entirely Jewish cocoon, to Richmond, the suburb immediately south of Vancouver, and into an environment of almost no Jews at all.

At school, I was sent to stand in the hallway, along with the Sikh kid in class, when the rest of the students recited the Lord's Prayer. Our next-door neighbour put up a poster facing our kitchen window telling us: "Jews go home. We don't want you here." My sister Stacey had a rougher time at school than I did, with elementary kids calling her a "dirty Jew" among other things. She had to change schools.

In retrospect, these experiences probably taught me to hide who I was. I was a social butterfly in school and I fit in well—but I sequestered my Jewish identity as best I could and mouthed the words to the Christmas carols, hiding the fact that I didn't know the words. I went through high school with little connection to my Jewishness—and showing even less of it to my peers.

In the summer after Grade 12, my parents pressured me to get a job as a camp counsellor. I had been an enthusiastic camper when we lived in Montréal and my parents may have seen a Jewish summer camp as a way to reinforce my increasingly fraying connections to my roots.

For many kids, summer camp is a formative experience. Having sublimated my identity as a Jew, this experience was liberating and life-altering.

Camp Miriam is a Labour Zionist summer camp for youth, magnificently situated on Gabriola Island, off the coast of Vancouver Island in the Salish Sea. Interestingly, it was purchased by the parent organization, Habonim Dror, from the Cooperative Commonwealth Federation, the precursor to the NDP, so there is an even deeper connection to my life history. There's another, more significant connection: When Leah Levi retired from leading the camp, my daughter Leya took over her role.

Camp Miriam was founded around the same time as the State of Israel and, since it is based on the collectivist model of the kibbutz, everyone, including the campers, participates in some of the decision-making. At Miriam, campers are responsible for one another and for parts of the camp itself, just as they would be if they lived on a kibbutz in Israel. Many decisions at the staff level and at the camper level are made collectively through consensus—even if that means sitting together for hours until a conclusion is reached. This is kind of like a cabinet or caucus meeting—although in our political system, the leader can usually call an end to the discussion and announce a decision. Among themselves, kids continue discussing until the decisions are made. It could turn into *Lord of the Flies*, but it doesn't.

I was hired as a camp counsellor in 1981. We had a two-week pre-camp training where I learned about child development, creating and running group activities, and leading by example. I learned how to work in a team, how to make collaborative decisions and how to ensure that campers under my care had a good time while also absorbing the lessons of collective responsibility.

It seems I was (and maybe remain) a camp counsellor at heart. I have carried the skills that I learned at Camp Miriam with me in myriad roles: as a parent (I know how to keep kids busy while waiting for our food to arrive in restaurants); as a family therapist (I know how to listen to everyone's perspective); and as a politician (you have to bring people along to come to a consensus and create change).

Leading young people and building a community and culture with them over the summer is not much different than working with adults in a workplace, on a City Council, in a caucus or cabinet. These are more complex communities and the issues are different, but the principles are the same. I learned that leadership is about showing, not telling. You lead by demonstrating to people what good leadership looks like.

The camp emphasized our connection with Israel as the homeland of the Jewish people and the role of Israel in ensuring the continuity, safety and security of Jews all over the world. It was the first time since leaving Montréal that I was surrounded by people who understood me—my values, my history, my culture, my outlook on life. Who I was. Who I am.

That summer was pivotal. It re-centred me in my identity after a time of upheaval. High school is always a time of finding, or inventing, oneself. Having been uprooted from an immersive Jewish environment and planted in a place where there was close to no Jewish life at the time (at least for me), Camp Miriam was a true homecoming.

I was reminded of the centrality of Judaism, of Jewishness, of the safety of community and the comfort that comes from being among people who you don't need to explain yourself to or hide who you are. I would never again let that go.

I spent four summers at the camp, building my knowledge and experience, and reconfirming my values and identity as a Jewish person.

While my introduction to Camp Miriam was positive and life-changing, my introduction to university . . . not so much.

The autumn after high school, I went to the University of British Columbia. It was a disastrous year for me academically. The university was too big and too impersonal for a 17-year-old who was just trying to figure out who she is in the world. Not only had I come from being a fairly big fish in the comparatively small pond of Richmond High, but I imagine I also suffered additionally because, at camp that summer, I had found a new sense of self.

I struggled through that first year at UBC and then told my parents I wanted to go to Israel for a gap year. Working on a kibbutz was an affordable way to travel and I had never been to Israel. Oh, and there was a boy that I liked who would be going to school there. (He broke my heart before I left for Israel, but I went anyway.)

My parents weren't thrilled with the idea of me taking a year off. They were concerned that I would never return to school. I would be the first person in our family to get a university education and they really wanted that for me. But I have always been someone who does what she wants. I appreciate parents who fear that a taste of the "real world" will sour their kids on post-secondary schooling, but I have also seen plenty of people who weren't ready for university right after high school, for whatever reason, so they dabbled in this or that, and then excelled when they began university later.

I spent just over five months on Kibbutz Ginigar, near Afula, in the north of Israel. As is typical, it included an *ulpan*, a work/study program focusing on language and culture. My jobs on the kibbutz included collecting eggs, working in the orange orchard, and milking cows.

After our chores, we would head to the classroom for two to three hours of Hebrew study. This was not the biblical Hebrew I studied as a kid. This was to learn modern conversational

Hebrew, a language that had been revived and rebuilt in the past century, alongside the modern State of Israel.

This time on my own, away from my family, away from everyone I knew, was transformative. Being on my own in a foreign country that also felt like home was a gift of independence that made all the difference to this 18-year-old kid who was looking to reconnect with herself and her identity. I truly found it.

After five months on the kibbutz, I joined an eight-week program called Livnot U'Lehibanot ("To build and to be built"). This was an innovative new program at the time, in which 20 young adults lived communally in Jewish Modern Orthodox tradition. We studied Jewish religion, thought and philosophy for half the day and helped rebuild the ancient city of Tzfat (Safed) the other half of the day. Tzfat is a magical place, the centre of Jewish mysticism and kabbalah, and a place where Jewish life has continued uninterrupted for thousands of years, even during the centuries of Jewish dispersion.

So much had been coming together to cement my connection to my Jewishness, but this experience further deepened my Jewishness. Living a full Jewish life in a Modern Orthodox framework while having easy access to rabbis and scholars who were on hand to answer (and help us answer) our questions was an irreplaceable gift.

Those eight weeks gave me an even stronger sense of which of my Jewish values was most important to me: *Tikkun olam*, making the world a better place.

Tikkun olam would become the guiding principle in everything I do. Tikkun olam determined my career choice, family therapy. It guided my efforts to strengthen communities through the social services sector. It was my North Star in elected life. It guided me through easy and tough decisions, including those involving my relationships, my health, carrying and bringing into the world three human beings—including one I carried as a surrogate for dear friends. It solidified in me the certainty of my life's path—if not the specifics of how my life would unfold, certainly the transcendent values that would be the rock upon which every decision was founded.

* * *

After I returned from Israel, I entered the "other" university in the Vancouver area, Simon Fraser University. By my logic, if I didn't have a great experience at UBC, I should try something else, so SFU was it. Besides, I had acquired eight Hebrew language credits from Haifa University and UBC refused to recognize them. SFU did, so that sealed it.

SFU was one of the many new universities that mushroomed across Canada in the 1960s, this one placed majestically atop Burnaby Mountain, to the east of Vancouver.

My gap year did wonders to ready me for university in a way I was not prepared for after high school. SFU was certainly a smaller campus, and the Socratic method of teaching, having tutorials in which small groups discuss readings, lessons and ideas—all under the leadership of a grad student—was a method that worked for me.

In my third year, I was introduced to the idea of family therapy. I learned that to become a family therapist, a graduate degree in counselling or psychology was required. I also learned that to get into grad school, you needed to have a high GPA, preferably an honours BA—and lots of volunteer hours.

My grades were pretty good, but I had to apply for the honours program. The other part was to gain volunteer experience. I started training with the Vancouver Crisis Centre's Youthline. It was a newly funded suicide prevention program and I was eager to contribute to helping people—it was tikkun olam, a way to help heal the world by making a difference for others while also fulfilling requirements that could lead to meaningful employment. I thought counselling seemed like the perfect career for me, helping people and making a living at the same time. Doing well by doing good.

The volunteer training was comprehensive and, in a few months, I was taking calls from people who needed someone to listen with empathy and help with resources or words of comfort. It was exactly as I had hoped it would be.

I got much more than I had bargained for. One of the other people in the January 1985 intake for training at the Vancouver Crisis Centre was a guy named Dan Robinson.

I didn't notice that he often signed up for shifts that overlapped with mine. It also didn't set off any alarms that Dan would be the one giving me a ride to the weekend training retreat that June at Evans Lake, near Squamish—and that no other volunteers were joining us for the drive.

It was years before Dan confessed to orchestrating the ride to Evans Lake, asking the retreat organizer to pair him up with me so that he could have time alone with me in the car. I wonder how contemporary readers will interpret this "How did you meet" story. Too stalky? I've chosen to find it adorable.

Things moved quickly—for Dan, especially. He started asking me to marry him just weeks after that trip to Evans Lake. I would laugh and remind him that he would just get in the way because I had things I wanted to do. One time, he responded with, "Who says we can't do the things you want to do together?"

That sealed the deal. A man who would join me in the life I wanted to create for myself. That seemed like the definition of a partnership. Isn't that what we all want? I had never met anyone like him. Yes, this man, Dan Robinson, was certainly an anomaly. And I was falling in love with him.

There was a problem, though. He wasn't Jewish.

While my Jewish identity had become even more central to who I was, I could picture a life with him whether he converted or not. Judaism traditionally recognizes matrilineal descent, so my children would be Jewish regardless of who their father was. We could raise the kids Jewishly and Dan could choose to be Jewish or not. I did not want to make it a condition of our marriage. It would be too one-sided and was not how I wanted to operate in our marriage, with ultimatums.

In October 1985, as we enjoyed a perfect dinner at Maiko Gardens, a lovely Japanese restaurant on Richards Street that sadly no longer exists, I looked at Dan and said, "You've asked me to marry you several times over the summer. I can see a future with you. Let's get married."

I'm a romantic fool, I know. Nevertheless, I swear he levitated off his seat.

We had to have conversations about The Jewish Thing. I knew that there would be lots of angst and questions from my parents. I had an aunt who "married out" and it did not go well for her. She converted to Catholicism and married in a church. None of the family was told, except my grandfather who secretly went to the wedding to "give her away." It became the family tragedy in a way, a story about a wayward sheep.

My generation was different, and I saw that there were some in the extended family who had "married out" and maintained happy and healthy connections with family. Besides, I was going to make sure to raise Jewish kids, so the issue of Jewish grandchildren, which my parents were certain to ask about, was settled.

At least that was my thinking. Dan's thinking was different. He wanted in.

The conversion for him was pretty significant. The learning part was fine. Dan knew how to study. He had finished his undergraduate degree and he was doing a fifth year at UBC, aiming for med school admission. (He tried. He didn't make it.) Instead, he went to graduate school and built a great career as a consulting ergonomist. But there was another unavoidable issue: Dan needed to get circumcised.

Circumcision is an outward sign of the eternal covenant between God and the Jewish people as set out to Abraham.

My dad was impressed. He said, "You must really love my daughter to do this."

We settled comfortably into married life and I completed my master's degree at SFU. I found my place almost immediately. As often happens in life, my career trajectory was not a straight line—and while family counselling has been the core of my work life, it also led to management roles in the social service sector as I rose through the ranks in the agencies where I worked. I was able to learn the ropes in a vast range of areas, including nonprofit governance, human resources, strategic planning, fundraising and budgeting—the gamut of the charitable social services sector. It was never boring. I enjoyed every aspect, but nothing was more meaningful or impactful than working directly with clients, assisting them in improving their lives, nurturing communication skills and enhancing their relationships through understanding.

As a family therapist, I had learned both formally and informally just how important it is to listen to people. If you expect to help people solve problems or feel better about themselves or their situation, you must be able to listen, not just with your ears, but with your heart as well.

These are skills that have served me well, especially in politics.

## *The fight of my life*

In my early 30s, I started running for regular daily exercise, to move my body and clear my mind. What began as a walk/run around the local park launched me on a journey that would take me through five or six half-marathons, two full marathons, two mini-triathlons and one 50-kilometre run on New Year's Day 2006. I was probably in the best shape of my life.

Several weeks into 2006, I noticed significant pressure in my lower left abdomen when I would bear down. It felt like something was in there. My GP at first suggested I might be experiencing pain or discomfort when ovulating. I assured her that I had been ovulating for 30 years and this discomfort was not ovulation. She sent me for an ultrasound.

The ultrasound showed that there was a small mass and it was suggested that this could be a fibroid attached to my uterus. Fibroids are non-cancerous growths on the inside or outside surface of the uterus. Approximately half of women will develop some fibroids by age 50.

In addition to having given birth to two children of my own, I had been a surrogate for a family who had tragically lost their first child. They had a second child but the birth of that child resulted in an inability to carry another pregnancy. As part of the surrogacy process, I had undergone several ultrasounds of my uterus a few years earlier and there was never an indication of fibroids.

Blood tests for cancer came back negative. The doctor was perplexed and suggested they biopsy the mass to determine what it was. As we got closer to the biopsy date, I asked if they could just remove the uterus and not simply do a biopsy. I didn't want to have to wait for another date to then remove the uterus or the mass. I was done having children—for me and for my friends—and I was ready to part with this piece of equipment that was causing me discomfort. My uterus had served me well, but I was ready to be done with it.

I was told that because they were not quite sure what the mass was, they advised an operation though my abdomen rather than a vaginal procedure. That was fine with me. I wanted this mass gone. I had already had three abdominal surgeries—C-sections—so I knew what the recovery would be like. I also took full advantage of this major surgery. I asked the doctor if she could tighten up the rectus muscles in the lower abdomen—a tummy tuck so to speak. These are the muscles that spread apart during pregnancy, and they don't come back together in quite the same way. Each subsequent pregnancy spreads these muscles further and further apart. I thought if I was going to go through a major abdominal surgery I might as well make the most of it!

When I woke up in recovery, quite dazed, I looked up and saw Dan and a few friends staring at me. I looked at my friend Ivan's face. Ivan is a GP and I could see the look of concern he had. Ivan should never play poker.

My gynecologist approached and I asked her, "How was your day?" She replied, "Not good." I then asked, "How was my day?" She said, "Not good."

She explained that when she opened up my abdomen she saw that the mass was not attached to my uterus. It was attached to the small bowel and was necrotizing. She took a biopsy and sent it off to histology, believing that this mass was a bowel cancer of some sort.

As a gynecologist, she had been prepared to perform a hysterectomy, but suddenly I required a bowel resection, something she was not trained to do. She was getting ready to close me up when she learned that in the next OR was a gastroenterologist who could do the procedure. She switched places with the gastroenterologist, she closed his patient while he came to resect six inches of my small bowel, remove the omentum and broad ligaments. Then my gynecologist joined the gastroenterologist and the two of them felt for small nodules or bumps that might be metastases along the many feet of small bowel I had left.

The histology came back positive for a gastrointestinal stromal tumor—GIST.

I had cancer.

I was 42 years old and in the best physical shape of my life. I had a wonderful marriage, two kids in high school and a decent middle-class life. I had worked hard to get here. I took care of my health. I never smoked. I ate healthy foods. I even trained for marathons. Despite all this, I got cancer. It wasn't fair. I had been doing all the right things and sometimes, sometimes even when you do the right things, bad things happen. This was a bad thing.

Not only did I need to heal from the invasive abdominal surgery, which I was fully ready for, but I now needed to deal with a severely disrupted gastrointestinal system that had been completely shut down. I would be in hospital for much longer than I had anticipated.

I imagined what it must have been like for Dan to get the news that I had cancer while I was unconscious and not mentally there with him. I imagined what it would be like for him, left alone to raise our two kids. I imagined what it would be like for my children, Aaron and Leya, at 16 and 14, faced with their mother's mortality. Even I hadn't yet faced that reality and my parents were in their 60s. This just broke my heart, their innocence robbed from them at such a young age. I didn't want them to know this grief just yet. I wanted them to have more time with the fantasy that being good and doing good led to good things.

As I continued to take stock of my life, which now seemed to be on a much shorter trajectory than I was anticipating, my mind turned to a meeting we had had with a financial planner just six months earlier. Given our desire to support our kids through their post-secondary education and the fact that our lifestyle required two incomes, the planner recommended that we purchase additional life insurance. We did—and thank goodness. Given the cancer diagnosis, I would no longer be eligible for affordable life insurance. Whatever happened, I knew that Dan would not have to worry about paying the bills if I died before our children graduated. They could maintain the life that we had worked so hard to create. It was one thing I didn't have to worry about. That decision is a profound testimonial for getting life insurance when your children are young. It was a tremendous relief to me.

I asked for copies of my hospital records so at least I had the reports from the two surgeons. They described my insides in great detail, though it was not terribly illuminating to a lay reader.

Ultimately, I could understand the bottom line: I had metastatic cancer. It was spreading from one part of my body to another.

Will I need more surgery? Is there chemotherapy? Will I need radiation? What kind of future will I have? Will these treatments make me sick? Will I be able to work? Will I live long enough to see my children graduate?

I focused on making sure that my kids understood what was happening. Given the easy access to the internet, I needed to make sure that they were getting accurate information, so Dan and I made a point of sharing everything we were learning about this cancer. Then we needed to share information with our social and support circle. It is a very big circle. Dan had already started an email group while I was in surgery to update family and close friends. As more people heard about my diagnosis, they asked to be included on the list. Our caring community expanded. Some brought meals, others drove the kids to their after-school programs. People just came to visit or helped out in other ways.

People truly cared and wanted to know what was happening. In addition to appreciating their concern, I had ulterior motives for keeping these people engaged. Should cancer kill me as a 42-year-old woman who was still actively parenting her children, I wanted these people to stay connected to my family, who would need additional support as they navigated their futures without me. Being open and honest with my social circle was a good investment for my family.

A month after surgery, I had another CT scan followed by my first oncology appointment a week later.

As Dan and I made our way to the BC Cancer Agency on 10th Avenue in Vancouver, we talked about our immediate future. Planning beyond six months felt futile. We had no idea what lay in store for me, or for us.

As we continued on the 45-minute drive, I said to Dan, "What if there is no more cancer? What if it's gone?" Dan responded, "That would be great." Ever the realist, he followed up with, "But the surgeon said she believes they did not get it all." We both knew that there was possibly another lesion that would require more surgery and possibly a colostomy.

As an insufferable optimist, I retorted, "I know. But if there is no more cancer, can we have a big-ass party to celebrate?" At this point, Dan would celebrate the slightest good news.

We met the oncologist, Dr. Meg Knowling, a kind woman who poked and prodded and started asking questions. I told her that I would answer her questions, but she first needed to answer mine. Did they see more cancer on the CT scan? There was no way I was going to report on how I was feeling until I knew how I was doing.

Her answer was that there was no evidence of any cancer on the CT scan. I was just fine.

Dan and I wept in each other's arms. It was the best news we could have imagined. Sometimes being an insufferable optimistic Pollyanna is also being a realist.

We pulled ourselves together and started making phone calls to children, parents, siblings and friends, telling everyone that there was no evidence of any remaining cancer and that we were having a party the following night and they should come with their hearts filled with hope.

I was prescribed Gleevec, generically known as imatinib, a targeted chemotherapy to keep the cancer at bay. I would be getting bloodwork and a CT scan every three months to monitor for any progression from the metastases. As a Canadian, one thing I never had to worry about was how we would pay for my medical care. This was not at all the case for Americans I encountered in online discussion groups, some of whom would have to pay $36,500 a year for the meds I would be on indefinitely. At that first party—and at every party when results came back clear—the first toast of the night was to Tommy Douglas, the New Democrat pioneer who, as Premier of Saskatchewan, introduced socialized medical care to Canada.

We usually hear "You have cancer" as a death sentence. And sometimes it is. I didn't want to hear it that way, so I focused on what was next. I set myself to living, not dying. In my mind, I had decided that I would live until I was at least 50 years old. Fifty felt like a long way off. In those eight years, my children would not just finish high school, but they would likely graduate from post-secondary schooling as well. I thought that if Dan and I continued to work hard, we might be able to pay off a big chunk of our mortgage and I felt like eight more years would give me time to do some of the things that I had yet to experience.

Eight weeks after surgery, I donned my running shoes and headed to run the Scotiabank Vancouver Half-Marathon. The surgery had significantly impacted my training regime, but I had signed up to do this race back in the fall and I still had the residual fitness from the 50-kilometre ultra-marathon I ran on New Year's Day. Cancer was not going to take this race away from me.

Dan and others did their best to dissuade me from "pushing myself too hard," but they also knew that when I set my mind to something it isn't easy to get me to change it. I promised that I would take it slow and walk as I needed to, but I was going to cross that finish line.

Dan had signed up as well and committed to run at my pace and make sure I didn't do anything stupid. I ran that race. It certainly wasn't my best time, but I was not going to let cancer stop me from doing the things that were important to me.

As I crossed the finish line, I burst into tears. It was the hardest race I had ever run, far harder than the 50-kilometre run I completed six months earlier. A lovely volunteer ran over with a wheelchair asking if I needed assistance getting to the medical tent.

"No, I don't need medical care," I declared. "I. Am. Just. Fine. I crossed that line on my own, thank you very much."

It probably came out more abruptly than I had wanted, but the fact that I could still run 26 kilometres on my own meant that I could get through whatever cancer had in store for me.

* * *

The BC Cancer Foundation's Tour de Cure was one of BC's biggest fundraisers for cancer research. (It no longer exists.) For me, this long-distance cycling event was a perfect example of tikkun olam.

I began my annual participation when I had overcome cancer (the first time). To me, it was a message of inspiration and hope from one survivor to another, to reassure them by example that a healthy future is absolutely possible.

Tour de Cure exemplified tikkun olam in another way. It created concentric circles of goodness. Everyone who participated inspired others. You could participate as a rider. You could donate money or volunteer. As a cancer survivor, you could do any of these things as a testament to the power of cancer research and medical advances. You could participate in honour of someone fighting cancer, in memory of someone, or as a celebration of someone who has survived. However you participated, it involved building communities of support—the sort of communities Dan and I built around us during my battles—and these circles often engaged their circles to make the world a better place in a multitude of small ways because one person took action. That to me is tikkun olam at its finest.

For years, my cancer treatment hummed along and so did I.

In June 2021, I had been on the chemotherapy for 15 years. I had made it past 50 and was heading to 60. I told my doctor that, while I was perfectly healthy, I worried that, with aging, my liver and kidneys could start to falter given the role they have in dealing with daily chemotherapy.

There was also a 15-year history with no evidence of disease and I had reduced the recommended dose by half. Perhaps I didn't have to take the medication? The oncologist suggested that I could stop taking it but I would need more regular CT scans to see if the cancer would make a reappearance.

After 15 years, I was going to cease this medication that slowed me down, gave me muscle cramps and prevented me from running (cramping calves while jogging are just not fun).

As it turns out, going cold turkey off the medication was bad advice. Within months, I had hip joint pain and mobility issues. I was Minister of Finance by this time, so I struggled to find time to address what was happening.

Over the years I fought cancer, I went through several oncologists. Most, like Meg Knowling, were outstanding in every way. The one who advised me to go cold turkey off my meds was not.

Soon my shoulders began to hurt, like someone was pulling my arms out of their sockets. I reached out to my oncologist, who wasn't particularly helpful. She didn't think my pain had anything to do with the sudden cessation after taking a drug every day for 15 years.

I tried every kind of joint relief medication and strategy possible. Finally, I had enough and asked for a different oncologist who immediately suggested that I go back on the chemotherapy. He sent me a new prescription and, lo and behold, it had warnings recommending that patients not stop taking the medication suddenly as that could create an inflammatory response in the hips and shoulders.

Sure enough, within 10 days of being back on the medication, the pain subsided. My new oncologist slowly weaned me from the chemotherapy so that I was drug-free and pain-free. He would now monitor my quarterly scans to make sure that I would remain cancer-free.

The first three scans were just fine. Then, in February 2023, he called to tell me that the latest scan showed that there was a tumour.

This could not be happening. Not again.

I crawled into Dan's arms and wept.

The doctor recommended that I return to my dose of 200 milligrams a day and said he would continue to scan me every three months. He reassured me that there are many treatment options if my body no longer responded to the imatinib. He reminded me that I had previously responded well and said he would work with me to find a treatment that worked. We would see if surgery was needed after I took the chemotherapy for several months.

I had to tell the kids, my dad, our extended family and friends. But now I was a cabinet minister. I had to share this publicly. I would have to make an announcement in a very public way so that I could control the story. The alternative would be a rumour mill. I needed to move fast, before word got out.

I called Premier Eby and told him of the diagnosis and my intent to share the news publicly that week. I focused on the positive—our superb healthcare system—and I invited everyone to join me in the BC Cancer Foundation's Tour de Cure fundraising cycling challenge.

The love and support I received from colleagues of all political stripes was heart-warming. Two members of the Legislative Press Gallery, CBC reporter Katie DeRosa and CHEK TV's Rob Shaw, both signed up to do the Tour de Cure with me and my team.

Rob and Katie hosted a legislative pie-tossing fundraiser and my colleagues from all sides of the Legislature gleefully participated, making financial contributions for the opportunity to throw a pie at a Press Gallery member. I delighted in covering legislative columnist Vaughn Palmer's face in whipping cream.

Several months later, I learned that the medication was working, the tumour size was shrinking. On October 6, 2023, just eight months after being put back on chemotherapy, I learned that the radiologist who reviewed my most recent CT scan could not detect a tumour. The chemotherapy that I had been on for 15 years was doing what it is supposed to do.

Dan and I went out for a celebratory dinner after making the requisite calls to our kids, parents and close friends. We had a delightful meal at a Thai restaurant near our home. We came home, tired but happy.

I turned on the TV and the world had changed. It was October 7 in Israel.

## *An Accidental Politician*

I NEVER PLANNED to enter politics. The first real engagement I had was speaking to Coquitlam City Council, my hands shaking, in support of an emergency cold weather refuge for homeless people proposed by a church in my neighbourhood.

After that inauspicious start, one of the councillors, Fin Donnelly, who would become a Member of Parliament and then a colleague of mine in the provincial government, suggested I run for Council the next year, in 2008.

I wasn't completely unfamiliar with local affairs. Neither was I entirely unknown to elected officials and others in the community. I was a family counsellor and worked at Share Family & Community Services as their Director of Fund Development. I was sometimes the smiling face in the local newspaper accepting the great-big cheques in those cheesy photos when donors contribute to good causes. I would frequent the Chamber of Commerce and other local events. But I was never set on a career in politics.

At the same time, I have always been open to new challenges. As much as I loved Share, and knew I was making a positive impact in the lives of our clients, I was getting a bit restless. I thought I could be a City Councillor and continue my work at Share, too.

I pulled some friends together and we organized a campaign. I began doing what I have learned to really enjoy—meeting people on the doorstep and finding out about their lives.

Throughout my political career, as it has developed, my background in family counselling has been an asset. I can hear what people are saying—and often what they are not saying. I can reframe a position to help people understand how a particular policy impacts their lives. I can empathize and sometimes drill down a little deeper to get at their motivation—like on that first campaign, when I was asking what issues were important to voters.

On the doorstep, one man thought for a moment and then declared that his top concern was the weeds in the cracks of the sidewalks. My first thought was, *Yikes, is this what municipal government is about?* But as I spoke to him more, it turned out his daughter was getting married soon and he would have lots of out-of-town visitors. This seemed like such a trivial issue but, for him, it was a point of personal and community pride. He wanted to show everyone he knew that he had provided well for his family as he sent his daughter out in the world. Understanding what drives people, even when it takes time to discover it, can be a valuable asset in connecting with them.

I am a tireless campaigner, partly because I really like meeting people and also because I hate to lose. I have enough self-awareness to recognize this in myself but this knowledge has not prevented a few overturned Scrabble boards in my day.

Running as an independent—there are no political parties on Coquitlam Council—means newcomers face an uphill slog. On the other hand, the profile I had in the community, combined with a lot of banging on doors, proved successful.

In our at-large system, the top eight vote-getters were elected to council—and I came seventh. I was a politician!

I had originally thought I could serve on Council and keep my day job. That may have been feasible, I came to realize, but it was not ideal.

Share receives funding from governments and financial support from business leaders including developers, those building the housing so desperately needed in our community. Issues directly impacting on the agency's work also come before Council now and then. I could—and would—recuse myself in situations like that, but I didn't like even the perception of a potential conflict. Plus, I wanted to be free to participate in everything Council considered. I suppose there was also a personality trait at play. When I decide to do something, I throw myself into it full bore. I became a full-time City Councillor (even if the pay was decidedly a part-time salary).

I loved my time on Coquitlam Council, learning everything I could about taxation, budget development, parks and recreation, community planning, transit, roads, policymaking, housing, infrastructure, and garbage collection. I engaged with community members on the things that mattered to them, and I learned how to work with people with varying perspectives and opinions. To me, this was a natural extension of my counselling work. It was also, in so many small ways, a constant reinforcement of my core Jewish value: repairing the world, making it a better place.

I ran again in the 2011 local election, using the same strategy as the first time, taking nothing for granted even though incumbency in local elections is a distinct advantage. I worked hard. This time I topped the polls for Councillor and was thrilled to dig into the work with a few new faces around the Council table.

I liked the Council atmosphere, where people could toss ideas around and consider them, regardless of where they came from, because there was no party discipline or partisan expectations.

* * *

Though not a fierce follower of any party, I certainly voted in every provincial and federal election, and pretty much always for New Democrats. As a family therapist, I saw up close the harm caused by BC Liberal policies after they came to power in 2001.

The Liberals hacked funding for agencies like the ones I worked with. (If you are not from BC, a note: "Liberal" was a misnomer for this right-wing party and it eventually changed its name, a rebranding so monumentally disastrous that it led leader Kevin Falcon to drop out of the 2024 election and effectively fold the party.) The BC Liberal governments under premiers Gordon Campbell and Christy Clark were often punitive, as though driven by cruelty. They harkened to an earlier time, of Ronald Reagan and Margaret Thatcher and former BC Premier Bill Bennett. Parallels with the Bennett years should have been no surprise because the BC Liberals were effectively the reincarnation of the old Social Credit party that had held a stranglehold on the province through much of the second half of the 20th century.

Diane Thorne was the New Democrat MLA for Coquitlam-Maillardville and she had decided against running for re-election in the 2013 provincial election. I was in my second term on Council and knew Diane not only through our shared public service but also through an almost identical career trajectory.

Diane had worked at Share Family & Community Services, served as a Coquitlam City Councillor and then was elected MLA in 2005. My career had been mirroring hers, and so perhaps she thought it logical that I should also become the MLA when she was ready for retirement.

She begged me to run in her place. I declined. I really like City Council, I told her.

I told Diane that the extra work and extensive travelling to Victoria didn't appeal to me. Diane insisted that being an

MLA was not much more work than City Council. We both knew that was a white lie.

Fin Donnelly, who had encouraged me to run for Council, was by this point a Member of Parliament, and he and Diane invited me to go for a walk. When we finished our stroll, I was thinking about it. But I wasn't persuaded.

Diane then asked what would help convince me.

"Do you want to meet Adrian?" she suggested.

Adrian Dix was the leader of the BC NDP at the time. He had been Chief of Staff to the BC NDP's Glen Clark, when Clark was Premier from 1996 to '99. At the height of a controversy that would eventually lead to Clark's resignation, Dix was fired after it was discovered he had backdated a memo to protect the Premier from a potential conflict of interest. Adrian had admitted his violation and, despite that, gone on to become MLA in Clark's old riding, one of the safest NDP seats in the province. Adrian was elected leader in a competitive race following a caucus implosion that led to the ouster of then-leader Carole James. Despite that bloody internal battle, the party had mostly reunified and by 2012 polls indicated Adrian was set to become the next Premier of the province.

In the summer of 2012, Adrian and I met at Diane's MLA office, which would eventually become my community office. Adrian seemed genuine but I wasn't wowed. He didn't seal the deal. He listened to my concerns and answered my questions. I don't even remember what I asked. I had a number of questions and ideas and Adrian ticked off a few of my items.

I did mention that I wasn't keen to participate in a nomination race. I don't want to sound entitled—if they had another candidate, I was happy to bow out. They were courting me, I wasn't pursuing this. I didn't want to run two campaigns in a short period, first for the nomination and then for the general election.

Moreover, I knew that nomination races can get ugly. I've always believed that family fights—that is, internal party races and conflicts—are the hardest part of politics. That would prove excruciatingly true for me a dozen years later. The partisan politics is comparatively easy. Intra-party politics gets personal and I didn't want to participate in that.

Diane and Adrian told me they didn't see any other candidates on the horizon and, even if other candidates did pop up, they and the party would put their weight behind me as Diane's chosen successor. I hadn't been vetted, but I knew there was nothing problematic they would find in my background.

I still didn't say yes.

A couple of weeks later, Dan and I took a long-planned vacation to Newfoundland. It happened that Diane Thorne and her husband Neil were there at the same time, as were Ellie and John Horgan. We all got together for drinks in a little pub in St. John's.

John Horgan, then-MLA for Langford-Juan de Fuca, near Victoria, had run against Adrian in the leadership race, placing third. Adrian eventually won by a sliver over Mike Farnworth. But we all expected Adrian to become Premier and it was not on anyone's mind then that John would soon replace Adrian as leader.

It was in this cozy little Newfoundland pub that John was able to speak to my heart. He understood what was important to me and enticed me in. He talked about making change for people.

John was an incredibly likeable person. His affection for others was palpable. He had a knack for getting to know people, understanding their motivations and speaking to them in a way that resonated. That would prove extraordinarily powerful when he put himself before British Columbians and people got to know him, as I began to in that St. John's pub.

John was curious about what motivated me and he seemed

to want to know how I tick. He identified what was important to me and then helped me understand what I could do at the provincial level to make things happen. I expressed my concerns about what I had witnessed while working in the social service sector and John pointed out that, as an MLA, I could help fix the parts of the system that appeared to be broken. That had me reflecting on different possibilities and fantasizing about what I could do. He talked about making the world a better place. He was talking my language. He was talking tikkun olam.

That was it. In a matter of weeks, I was in.

## *A tough campaign*

My first impressions of the provincial party were a bit disheartening. The NDP has a reputation for grassroots vitality. The right-wing "establishment" parties might have the money, but the NDP has always been seen as the party of community organizing and on-the-ground strength.

If "grassroots" implies "down-to-earth," the dumpy, cluttered party headquarters lived up to the billing. The basement was filled with discarded old computer terminals and printers.

They had not yet professionalized the operation, although I give enormous credit to Craig Keating, the eventual party president and a fellow City Councillor (from the City of North Vancouver), who worked with us post-2013 to haul the party into the 21st century.

I understood that grassroots organizing happens in communities, it doesn't happen in a building. So I didn't take the state of the party office as anything particularly ominous. Although maybe I should have.

A major reason for the apparent chaos, certainly, was the recent history of the BC NDP. After a decade in office, the party had been almost entirely demolished in the 2001 election. After two terms in government, the NDP was routed 77-to-2 by the BC Liberals. Only Joy MacPhail and Jenny Kwan survived the tsunami.

I wasn't in the party at that time, but when you experience such an overwhelming loss, I am sure the entire foundations that had been built drop away.

Joy and Jenny did their best to provide an opposition to the landslide Gordon Campbell government, a colossal burden I cannot imagine. The BC Liberals almost immediately set about attacking everything that is important to progressive voters.

In the succeeding years, the NDP had undertaken the rebuilding process admirably. Carole James, who was party leader from 2003 to 2010, took on the unenviable task of transforming the party and now the NDP was poised to replace the Liberals. Some polls even suggested a rout on the magnitude of 2001, reversing the humiliation the Liberals had dealt to the NDP.

Of course, in a testament to the party's capability for turning on their own that perhaps should have given me pause, it would not be Carole set to lead the party into that prophesied Promised Land of government, but Adrian.

Carole is an extraordinarily talented woman who doesn't get the kudos she deserves for what she did for the party and the province. In what still awes me as an act of unbowed courage and determination—and loyalty to ideas shared by colleagues who demonstrated no personal loyalty to her—Carole went on to serve as a superb Minister of Finance when we finally returned to government.

When I arrived on the party's doorstep in 2012, there was still plenty of work to do to rebuild. In fact, it turned out, there was more work to do than we had imagined, and we'd have more time to do it, a fact that became disappointingly clear the next year, when we snatched defeat from the jaws of victory.

* * *

Being a provincial candidate after being a municipal official was not a difficult transition. For one thing, I agreed wholeheartedly with what we were proposing in our party platform, so while a move from municipal to provincial politics involves some loss of independence, it can be a fair trade-off. I was fighting for things that were important to me. I knew we would make the province a better place and repair some of the damage done to our social fabric over 12 years of Liberal rule.

As an independent City Councillor, you need to learn, as best you can, the details of everything that comes before you. At senior orders of government, you are part of a team. One benefit is that you have access to some of the best minds on every issue.

Do I know a lot about greenhouse gases? I understand why we need to reduce emissions, but I have to trust people who know the science and have a thought-out plan for confronting this existential problem. It's a team sport and you have to trust your crew. I was fully on board with our environmental plan.

I never struggled with our childcare plan, knowing from personal experience the challenges working parents face. I wanted something better for the next generation.

As a family counsellor and a City Councillor, I saw the impacts of unaffordable housing. As someone with (too much) experience in the healthcare system, I knew some of the strengths and weaknesses there, too. The BC NDP had a platform that really spoke to my values. These were all things I knew I could enthusiastically campaign on. It never felt difficult.

At the start of the campaign, Adrian declared that we would run a positive campaign. I liked the sound of this because I had told him at the outset that I didn't want to do "ugly politics."

The problem, it appeared, was that Adrian didn't seem to know what it meant to run a successful, "positive" campaign. Running a positive campaign means not slinging mud at the other party, taking low blows, or engaging in personal attacks. But it doesn't mean withholding comments around bad policy.

I'd like to believe that I haven't engaged in ugly personal politics. But that isn't the same as criticizing specific policies. Focusing on policies was, at a minimum, essential to convey that we did not want more of the BC Liberals' undermining social programs. The attacks the BC Liberals engaged in on services to the most vulnerable, including neglecting the housing crisis, cutting funds for rape crisis centres and refusing to increase welfare rates, deserved thorough condemnation. That's about policy, that's not about personalities. That's clear to me. It didn't seem to be clear to Adrian sometimes. It was as though he wasn't willing to prosecute the 12-year record of the BC Liberal government, a period of some of the most regressive policies any jurisdiction in Canada has ever seen. There was so much to condemn, to litigate, to illuminate as things that could be done better. And it seemed that Adrian let one opportunity after another slip through his hands.

A seemingly insignificant but telling detail gave me pause very early on. Brian Topp was selected as provincial campaign manager. At that point, I had not been immersed in this stuff, but Brian had run for the federal NDP leadership. He was a party organizer, and I'm not sure that the roles of organizer and the role of leader necessarily demand the same skill set. I'm sure some people have the talents to bridge those respective demands but I'll admit to having doubts.

This may not sound like a big deal and perhaps if things had gone differently I would have forgotten this detail. But I sussed Brian out a little bit online. I remember scrolling through the Facebook page from his federal leadership race. It was pages and pages long, but it was not the way you use social media effectively. It wasn't engaging people, it was talking at them, bombarding them with what amounted to political advertising. That our campaign manager did not understand how to use social media—and perhaps more telling, did not have the facility to seek out experts who did—was a red flag. Again, if things had not gone off the rails, this might have been a forgettable detail. Instead, when the dust settled, an exhaustive post-mortem of the campaign could be summarized as: Anything that *could* go wrong *did* go wrong.

But that was in the future. So confident was the party at the start of that campaign that we were aiming for a landslide.

We were not, though, up against Gordon Campbell. After a tumultuous decade, Campbell had resigned. The leadership, and the premiership, had been taken over by Christy Clark.

Clark was a known quantity, having served in top portfolios under Campbell. She had taken leave from politics but kept herself very much in the public eye—or ear—as a radio hotline host, a favourite side gig for retired (or sabbatical-taking) BC politicians. Having sat out the last term of Campbell's regime, she could return as a comparatively fresh face.

While Adrian had promised a "positive" campaign, the Liberals launched one of the nastiest in a province with a history of tough campaigning. They threw the kitchen sink at us.

Even though the Liberals had been in power for more than a decade and had a record that we should have been able to eviscerate, they managed to put us on our back foot, attacking the records of the Mike Harcourt and Glen Clark NDP governments of the previous century.

One of the most effective lines of attack was reminding voters that Adrian had been fired for his backdating of the memo while in the Premier's Office. That was a hard accusation to deflect. It spoke to people's understanding of his character.

There were many disasters in that campaign—weird moments that would become memes in a time when the word meme hadn't quite reached the zeitgeist—but the bottom line was that Adrian simply wasn't a great campaigner.

This is not necessarily an irredeemable fault. Some people are great campaigners and bad at governing. Some people are great at governing but not awesome campaigners. I think Adrian demonstrated, when we finally returned to government, that he is in the latter category as he proved when, as Minister of Health, he led the province through the COVID pandemic.

I was not an incumbent, of course, but I was running in an NDP riding. I thought I was going to win. Everyone assumed I was a shoo-in. From the early days of the campaign there was no assumption that incumbent New Democrat MLAs were endangered. We were looking to pick up great swaths of new seats and returning to the Legislature with an enormous caucus.

The riding had been an NDP stronghold for some time, with the exception only of the 2001 Liberal landslide. Of course, you don't take things for granted. I was door-knocking morning to night, attending every gathering of voters I could find. But I could feel a shift on the doorstep. In fact, I can pinpoint the exact moment.

Kinder Morgan had proposed a $5.4-billion twinning of an oil pipeline from Alberta to Burnaby, where the oil would be shipped to Asia. The route runs right through Coquitlam, as well as through many other BC communities. Adrian had committed to waiting until after Kinder Morgan submitted a formal proposal and environmental assessments were completed before determining whether we would support the project. Fair enough. The unions whose workers would benefit from the project were supportive. Many environmentalists, who thought we should be investing in alternatives, not expanding exports of non-renewable resources, were opposed. Adrian was walking a line but I think it was a good policy. Why jump the gun on a decision before all the information is in?

It was dinnertime. I was on the doorstep talking to a voter about the pipeline. The resident told me, "Your leader opposes the pipeline." I said, no, and explained the nuanced position the party had taken, waiting for environmental reviews before deciding, which was the prudent thing to do.

"No," the gentleman insisted. "I just saw him on the news. He's opposing the pipeline."

I couldn't believe it. Candidates have our speaking notes on all these issues. There were NDP candidates like me, all out banging on doors sharing that message, a well-considered, carefully crafted platform developed over months. And I had to hear from a voter that my leader had spontaneously reversed our position on a core plank.

I felt humiliated that I didn't know what I was talking about. And I was angry. I'm out on the doorstep and the leader and the party didn't have the decency to give those of us who were running any advance warning. How can you change positions on a foundational policy in the middle of the campaign without telling anyone? I had no experience on how a provincial campaign is run, but I knew this couldn't be right. The leader didn't communicate with us, he certainly didn't consult. He responded in the moment in a knee-jerk way. And for what? Why shift now?

I wouldn't say that the pipeline was the top concern for people in my constituency. Voters in my riding, and probably in every riding, were most concerned with education and healthcare, housing affordability and other pocketbook issues. The pipeline was a pocketbook issue for many union households—and the new position cost us votes in plenty of ridings, especially in the interior—and it was top of mind for some environmentalists. But, at least until then we could have played both sides of the fence (not always a courageous position but in this instance absolutely fair, I think). But that wasn't the main problem.

What became the ballot issue was what that flip-flop said about Adrian Dix as a leader, that he would summersault on an issue like that.

The Liberals had already hammered his integrity with the memo scandal. Now they came out with ads showing Adrian's head on a weathervane, shifting with the winds.

People who cannot wrap their minds around the complexities, advantages and disadvantages of a multi-billion-dollar oil pipeline project can easily recognize a leader who appears to make decisions on the fly.

A campaign in which everything was going right might have been able to withstand a blunder like this. For a campaign where everything was pretty much going wrong, it was a death knell.

After the flip-flop, people started to tell me, "We really like you, but we don't like your leader." I had never heard that until after the pipeline fiasco. There was nothing I could say that could counter that message on the doorstep.

This is when a structural problem in the campaign became really clear to me.

I tried to feed what I was hearing back to the central campaign. But there was no mechanism to do so. I got the message in no uncertain terms that the communication channels went one way only.

## *From the jaws of victory*

Election night 2013 was incredibly stressful. As the polling stations reported vote counts, I was neck and neck with the BC Liberal candidate, Steve Kim. This was not how the night was supposed to unfold.

A mere month earlier, when the campaign had begun, candidates like me, in what were assumed to be safe NDP ridings, were supposed to be celebrating with our volunteers, toasting victory and watching the bottom of the TV screens as our party racked up one win after another in places we have never been successful before. This was supposed to be a landslide.

By the end of the campaign, we had given up hope of a landslide. The Liberals had run a vicious, take-no-prisoners campaign while we had run a pitiable operation. Regardless, the poll numbers had been so sky-high for us at the start that even dropping precipitously in the polls still left us in good stead to win.

Steve, my Liberal opponent, is a lovely man who seemed to agree with pretty much everything I had to say at all-candidates meetings. Steve's parents were also delightful. They lived in the riding and at one all-candidates meeting they approached me apologetically, saying that while they voted for me for council, they would be voting for their son in this election. I laughed and assured them they should absolutely be supporting their son, that he was an impressive young man and that they should be very proud of him for putting his name forward. In retrospect, I may have betrayed a little overconfidence. Steve did more than "put his name forward." He beat me on election night!

The lead kept switching throughout the evening. One poll would come in and push me into the top spot, then another would be tallied and Steve would be up a few votes. It went on like this all night. When all the ballots were counted on election night, I lost by 105 votes.

I was devastated. I am not someone who places blame on others when things don't go right for me. Part of the reason I'm not a good loser is because I beat myself up over real or perceived failures.

In this instance, though, I did project a little. And I think it was fair to do so.

Our parliamentary system and our political traditions put a lot of emphasis on the party leader. Formally, provincial election voters are choosing an MLA. But most voters cast their ballot less on who their local candidate is than on the party or the leader they would like to see elected.

I worked incredibly hard in that election and I thought I would win. But when the party leader loses the confidence of voters around the province, local candidates lose votes.

Anyone who watched the nightly news knew the BC NDP had run a bad campaign. The leader had to—and did—take blame for that. As a candidate at the local level, I saw up close how bad the campaign was and how that trickled down to make my work harder—and led, ultimately, to my defeat on election night.

Thankfully, when the numbers were down for me, my campaign manager Tania Jarzebiak pulled me aside. She assured me that we were not conceding the election just yet. I had lost in the election night count, but there were absentee ballots to be counted. And there were a lot of them—about 2,000—that would be tallied in the next two weeks and New Democrats traditionally do well in absentee ballots.

In British Columbia, you can be in Prince George or Victoria and vote for the candidate in your home riding of Coquitlam-Maillardville or Kootenay-Rockies. It took two (agonizing) weeks for those to be counted, because they all went to a central clearinghouse, were divided by ridings and then forwarded to the local returning office. Partly because New Democrat voters tend to be committed to the cause and partly because we have a good ground game (usually), we can depend on doing better than the other parties in these ballots. Though, of course, nothing is certain—as the province-wide results were telling us that night.

With just 105 votes separating me from Steve, I still had a chance. We would wait until all the votes were counted.

While I was facing my own drama on election night in 2013, at least I went to bed with some hope that outstanding ballots might turn things around and send me to the Legislature. At the province-wide level, there was no such hope for the party.

The NDP, when all the results were in, had not gained the MLAs we had hoped, but actually lost two seats, declining in the popular vote from the previous election. Christy Clark and her BC Liberals had achieved one of the most dramatic comebacks in political history.

People were stunned, absolutely shocked—no matter which side they were on. BC Liberals were astonished and ecstatic. New Democrats were astonished and devastated. The atmosphere at our local "victory party" was morose. I suppose if I had won my riding, we could have taken a little solace that night, but we didn't even have that.

Dan and I slunk back home. Fin Donnelly, at the time our MP, came over, joined by my campaign manager Tania. Fin was swearing a blue streak—and he spoke for all of us that night. We were all just shaking our heads.

I went back to my Council duties as best I could. I rode my bike, gardened, and waited. And waited.

The count of the absentee ballots was on a Monday—a Council day. I sat in committee meetings, squeezing the hand of my colleague and friend Mae Reid as my phone would vibrate with updated counts. It took hours to count the absentee ballots. I would get texts like "You are only down 80 votes." Then an hour later, I would get a text saying, "You are only down 28 votes." Then eventually the numbers changed "You are up by four ballots," and then "You are up by 19 ballots." The final absentee ballots were counted around 8 PM that evening. I was up by 35 votes!

Call me Landslide Robinson.

It was an unbelievable feeling. I had adjusted my expectations to prepare for defeat. I had tasted defeat, on election night. But now, two very long weeks after the election, I was victorious.

I was delirious.

Because of the ridiculously narrow margin of 35 votes out of almost 22,000 ballots, it automatically went to a judicial recount, so there would be one final hurdle. But to topple me from victory at this point would require a judge to disallow 36 NDP ballots—and find no discrepancies on the other side. The odds were strongly in my favour and the final judicial recount declared me the winner by a whopping 41 votes.

I was the new MLA for Coquitlam-Maillardville.

## *On to Victoria*

When I got to Victoria, I found my footing pretty quickly. I was the person in high school who hung with the smokers in the parking lot, the jocks in the gym, the theatre kids in the drama room and even in the principal's office, not because I was in trouble but because I liked chatting with adults. I've always been pretty good at finding my place in groups.

This was handy because I didn't have roots in the party. I did not become a signed-up member of the NDP until I decided to run. I also do not come from the union movement, as many New Democrats do.

Arriving at the Legislature was exciting and new for me, though of course it was a disappointment to be on the opposition side of the House. That wasn't as devastating for me as it was for some of my colleagues who had been in opposition since 2005 (or, in Jenny Kwan's case, since 2001). I was a neophyte who had to learn the ropes, figure out how to work in a partisan environment, make sense of parliamentary procedure and navigate the workplace politics as 85 of us toiled to make life better for British Columbians. Opposition is a more comfortable place to learn these lessons than the higher-stakes government side of the House.

Still, opposition is not the role most candidates aspire to, although many find a footing as powerful voices holding the government accountable. Our role was to point out the government's shortcomings, and there were plenty of those.

I asked to take on the critic role for municipal affairs, which Adrian gladly gave to me since it's probably not a file that everyone covets. I loved local government and recognized its role in providing critical services to communities. The BC Liberal government did not have a great relationship with local governments, so I knew that we could make some friends in those circles. When John Horgan became leader, he added the seniors file and then the mental health and addictions responsibilities to my critic portfolios. I learned all I could about these areas so I could hold government to account and so I would be as prepared as possible should we have the opportunity to form government.

As much as I loved learning my new role as an MLA, I quickly discovered that even the best ideas in the world, if they come from the opposition, will likely never get considered. I came to understand that Question Period is a performance for the Press Gallery. The goal is to shine a light on an issue that you want the media to cover so that British Columbians become more aware of what their government is doing, or not doing.

Being in opposition gave me time to learn before being thrown into the maelstrom of government. I think it also gave me some humility and empathy for my "esteemed colleagues across the way," as we say in the Legislative Chamber, when we finally moved to the government side of the House.

There was to be a maelstrom on our side of the House soon enough, though. The shocking loss in the election meant that Adrian resigned as leader. Hardly had we reconvened in Victoria than we were thrown into a wide-open leadership race.

## *Family fight*

A few people suggested that I should run for leader. I told them I should maybe figure out where the washrooms are before I try to run the place. I didn't even know how laws were made back then and I had never set foot in the Legislature before becoming an MLA.

Not only would I not be running for leader, but I would try to remain as remote from the fray as possible. As I have said, I didn't know a lot about partisan politics but I knew that these internal party contests and related disagreements were among the bloodiest aspects of the game. There is no fight like a family fight.

David Eby was the first out of the gate. It was a gutsy move—like me, he was elected for the first time just a couple of months earlier. David was a giant-slayer because, while Christy Clark snatched victory from the jaws of defeat to win the election province-wide, David bested Clark in her West Side Vancouver riding of Point Grey. That was one bright light for New Democrats on that bleak election night. Clark would later run in a by-election in the Okanagan and return to the House as Premier.

David is a lawyer who was already well-known as a non-profit leader at Pivot Legal Society, which advocates for BC's most marginalized populations, and more recently he had been Executive Director of the British Columbia Civil Liberties Association. He was also an adjunct professor at UBC.

David asked for my support and I told him I would wait to see who was running before making a decision. Then Mike Farnworth said he was interested. Mike is my neighbouring MLA and I've known him a long time because the Tri-Cities communities, Coquitlam, Port Coquitlam, Port Moody, Anmore and

Belcarra, are very close and we would often be at the same community events. Then John Horgan reluctantly threw his hat in the ring. John was the one who convinced me to run provincially. He had found the key to unlock my resistance, convincing me that this was the next avenue for me to live out my vision of tikkun olam, of repairing the world.

On top of that connection, Adrian had assigned John the role of House Leader, which meant he was to negotiate with the government side on what was being debated and how to best use the allotted time that we have for debate. John understood how the place worked and had deep appreciation and respect for the legislative process. Throughout that first legislative session after the election, John would come into my office and say, "Hey Robinson, how's it going?" He just wanted to hear what the newbie thought, felt, wondered about. I really appreciated that. I don't know if he was doing it because he was House Leader or because he was my friend but I felt like he really cared about me. He would provide words of wisdom or comfort. It was often just a three-minute sit-down and then he would move on because House Leader is a busy role. But those occasional check-ins meant the world to me.

David soon dropped out of the leadership race because his partner Cailey had become pregnant. I told him you only get to be a first-time dad once. He was young and there would be another time for him, I said. Now it was just John and Mike in the race. John had lots of endorsements from sitting MLAs. Everyone liked John. I really like Mike and, as I said, he was my neighbouring MLA, so many thought I would endorse my local guy for leader.

You wouldn't necessarily know it, but Mike is kind of a shy guy. I don't hold that against him. It's just who he is. But having just come through an election with Adrian Dix, I was pretty emphatic that, since we had already tried a shy guy, a gregarious, outgoing leader who clearly enjoys being around people seemed like a better bet.

I know it hurt Mike when I told him that I would be supporting John's candidacy for leader.

While I don't doubt that Mike could be a good Premier, I wasn't convinced that he would get the chance, having seen somebody with a similar personality crash and burn in the election we had just come through.

The family fights I had feared were quick in coming. There was some nastiness in the Twitterverse, some pseudonyms attacking me for backing John over Mike. These were New Democrats slamming me on social media and I was pretty sure I knew who they were.

I asked Mike if it might be some of his supporters going rogue and asked if he could get them to stop. It ended immediately.

While I have always liked Mike, I have come to absolutely admire him. He was hurt and upset with me for a while and it did impact our friendship for a time. But we became incredibly good friends over the years. He is my go-to guy on so many things, like how to handle a difficult situation with a colleague, sort out a concern with the media, or for advice on how to approach an intergovernmental issue. He's been an incredible support for me through the worst of what I have experienced. He's probably been the most loyal to me at a time when I felt so betrayed and abandoned by so many.

John had tremendous support from sitting MLAs and Mike was fighting an uphill battle. After I announced my endorsement for John, Mike dropped out of the leadership race and John became leader by acclamation.

Once the new leader was in place, I dove into my opposition critic roles, partly because that's what I do and partly out of the confidence that, having missed out on being elected government in 2013, our party would be victorious next time. I was determined to gain as much expertise on my files as I could so that, if given the chance, I would be an asset on the government side of the House.

The opportunity would come—but not without a lot more drama and unanticipated twists and turns.

# *Power and Pandemic*

I WOULD INDEED get to take the skills and knowledge I gained in opposition over to the government side. The 2017 election turned out to be British Columbia's first minority government in 65 years. It was an unbelievable squeaker. Christy Clark, who had managed to overturn every prediction four years earlier to win her first full term as Premier, was defending her record.

In Coquitlam-Maillardville, while I knew far better than to take anything for granted, we didn't have to wait long on election night for the good news. Unlike the previous election, when I lost on election night but won on the absentee ballots, this time I was elected easily, with more than half the votes cast.

At the province-wide level, it could hardly have been closer. Clark's Liberals held 43 ridings. Under John Horgan, the NDP gained six, to take 41 seats. Andrew Weaver's Green party tripled their seat count—from a single seat to three—putting them in the enviable position of kingmaker (or queenmaker). It was up to the Greens to determine who would form government.

As she had done throughout her career, though, Christy Clark refused to go down without a fight.

The Greens negotiated a supply and confidence agreement with the New Democrats that would make John Horgan head of an NDP government. This was not a coalition government—it was an agreement that the Greens would support the government on confidence votes in return for specific actions on climate, poverty reduction, childcare and a raft of other progressive policies.

Despite the writing on the wall, Clark insisted on going forward, convening the House, delivering a Speech from the Throne and then, as everyone knew would happen, watching her government get defeated in a confidence vote.

John Horgan met with the Lieutenant Governor and was asked to form a government. I cried happy tears.

John asked me to become Minister of Municipal Affairs and Housing. I was thrilled to take this on in government. The housing file, in one of the world's most unaffordable jurisdictions, was no small assignment. The new Premier also gave me responsibility for Translink, Metro Vancouver's transit network, so I had a full plate.

I had another responsibility that wasn't in my formal job description.

In opposition, I had become a conduit between the Jewish community and the BC New Democratic Party and caucus. I was tasked by the party to help them understand the Jewish community and ensure that we, the New Democrats, were present at important Jewish community events. In government, that role would be magnified. Now that I was a member of government, Jewish British Columbians came to me for guidance in dealing with policy issues or seeking help with problems. In Canada, larger ethnocultural communities often have at least one individual in government who acts as a point person for their issues. There have not always been openly identified Jews elected to the BC Legislature, and so our community has sometimes not had that personal connection on the inside. I took on this informal role, committed to building a stronger bridge between government, the NDP and the Jewish community.

I believed that what we were doing as a party and a government was the right thing for our province and so it was my honour to explain that work to my fellow Jewish British Columbians and encourage them to support us. John Horgan could not have been a better partner in this effort. When there was an opportunity for John to join with the Jewish community at an event, he would always seek my counsel to confirm that he understood the issue, the proper tone and the impact it had on Jews. He trusted me to provide him with good advice and I strove to do that at every opportunity. After I explained to him the Jewish concept of being a "mensch"—literally a "man" but figuratively an awesome human being of any gender—John would come to me or text me after an event asking if he did OK. He would almost always sign off by asking "Was I a mensch?"

And he always was.

That bridging role would take on unanticipated significance when an unprecedented epidemic of antisemitism swept Canada and the world. But before that, there was a pandemic of a different kind we did not foresee.

* * *

None of us anticipated a health crisis that would affect every person on the planet.

I think when future historians look back, they will marvel at how the world responded to the COVID pandemic. There are greater and lesser success stories, and tragedies beyond measure. The human impacts were devastating—both in terms of lives lost and the grief caused to families and communities, but also in the social effects on kids who lost learning and social opportunities and all of the other effects COVID had on each of our lives, whether or not we or our families were directly affected by the virus itself.

Economically, though, Canada and other Western jurisdictions, while adopting a range of approaches, managed to stave off what could have become the worst economic disaster since the Great Depression—or maybe ever. How soon we forget that the entire world shut down. Global productivity plummeted in an instant.

Governments were accused, by some, of shovelling money off trucks. That is a shallow way of characterizing what happened. There is no doubt that some people profited and others got funds to which they weren't entitled. But however much money might have been misallocated in the grand scheme, it was a relatively small price to pay for preventing the global (or national or provincial) economy from going off a cliff.

Responses to the pandemic were a model (in most cases) of the potential and importance of good government. This was an example of how governments can step up in the most important moments. It shouldn't need to be said that responding to a global pandemic isn't something you can leave solely to the private sector.

When the pandemic struck and the world shut down, in 2020, it affected all aspects of my file, as it did almost every facet of life on earth. My portfolios were especially central in responding at a "people level" to the crisis.

There are almost 200 local governments in BC, and all of them were depending on my department for guidance. They needed help making decisions to keep everyone safe. They required assistance to coordinate their messages, to ensure they were consistent with medical advice, and several of the mayors needed significant help managing anxiety in their communities (as well as their own anxieties, in some instances).

Mayors and councils had to decide what to do with their community centres, their parks and playgrounds. Should they remain open? Under what conditions?

There were also logistical and legal hurdles. The Local Government Act, under which they operate, required in-person attendance at municipal Council meetings. We needed to give them the legal and technological tools to meet and make decisions online, and to ensure they always had the most up-to-date public health information to make sound decisions.

We knew that as parts of the economy either slowed or closed entirely, people would be challenged to pay rent or cover the mortgage. We needed to come up with a plan that included temporary measures that could keep people housed and landlords above water.

While those who could work from home transitioned to the newly discovered technology of Zoom, we needed to keep transit operating so that essential services could keep running. Not only members of healthcare teams, but long-term care workers, grocery store employees and others depend on transit to get to work. We needed to find a way to keep that system up and running even as ridership completely tanked.

My initial focus was the housing file. We needed to make sure that we could keep people housed, even if they couldn't pay rent. And we needed to do it quickly. We had to make sure we had a system in place that worked for everybody. We temporarily changed regulations so that tenants weren't evicted for non-payment of rent. It also meant that we needed money from the treasury and we needed to develop a program that permitted us to get rent directly to landlords. Additionally, it meant asking those who could pay rent to continue to do so.

We had weeks, not years, to develop a brand-new program that could deliver for vulnerable tenants, many of whom had never in their lives viewed themselves as economically vulnerable and certainly not housing insecure. It was a Herculean effort made by the folks at BC Housing and my team of public servants at the Ministry of Municipal Affairs and Housing, who never lost sight of what we were trying to accomplish.

In addition to those at risk of homelessness, we were also incredibly worried about those who were already unhoused. They were at particular risk for COVID, given their often-compromised health and the close quarters of our traditional shelter model, which would put everyone at risk for contracting the disease. We needed a plan and we needed to move fast.

We purchased motels and other buildings to accommodate precariously housed or unhoused individuals. We "thinned" our shelter model to reduce the risk of contracting the disease by reducing the number of residents per shelter. We moved mountains and it felt like it was never enough. Even before COVID, it was difficult to get housing built quickly and to get unhoused people into safe, appropriate shelter. Now, here we were working as quickly as we could to open thousands of additional units and we were running out of trained staff and not-for-profit partners with the capacity to do what we needed to accomplish.

Closer to home, over a frantic weekend in March 2020, Dan and I turned my adult son's former bedroom into a ministerial office and that is where I spent most of the early weeks of the pandemic. I went from my bedroom to the kitchen, to my home office and typically stayed there for 10 to 12 hours every day. At 3 PM daily, I made a cup of tea as I tuned in to watch Dr. Bonnie Henry, the Provincial Health Officer, give the latest update to the public. As a cabinet and a caucus, we would often get briefed separately earlier in the day, but it was important to know what the public was hearing so that I could continue to support my constituents and staff accordingly.

The information about COVID was constantly changing, making it particularly difficult for governments. Communicating health advice, public policy measures and programmatic changes to five million people when the message at the end of the week was different from the message at the beginning of the week was a huge challenge.

I instituted weekly calls with local governments, organized by region. Different regions were being impacted differently by the virus and the various levels of closure. As a government, we also needed on-the-ground intelligence. What were communities experiencing? What were their greatest needs? What were the greatest gaps? How could the province help? What did we need from the federal government?

We divided the province into five governing regions. Every Thursday, we spent an hour with mayors or their designates from each region. Each had three to five minutes to share a priority or two after I had given them the latest updates. Ministry staff on the line would track questions and information for follow-up. On occasion, I would have Adrian Dix, the Health Minister, on the call so local leaders could hear directly from him. At the end of every Thursday, I would review what we had heard and identify themes that could help us understand how government programs were working (or not working). I was then able to share what I was hearing from all around the province with the Premier and cabinet. It was a draining process, but necessary to support local leaders and to know what was happening in BC communities.

It was through this process that it became clear that communities without high-speed internet access were being left behind. Those who were still on dial-up were at an unacceptable disadvantage. Necessity being the mother of invention, we were seeing businesses and post-secondary institutions creating online systems, which we recognized as having significant potential for future educational and economic opportunities for British Columbians, including First Nations communities, in rural parts of our province. It became glaringly apparent, if it wasn't already, that we needed to invest in this critical infrastructure. It was this experience that solidified my commitment to invest millions for rural high-speed internet when I became Finance Minister.

COVID was hard on everybody. We were all living with the unknown. We had to trust a science that was continually evolving. We had to trust government leaders who didn't have a manual on what to do in case of a pandemic. We were forced to adapt to an always-changing landscape, where yesterday's advice was no longer relevant, and for months and months we had to make decisions based on new information. The rate of change was relentless.

We had to learn to trust others to keep us safe, whether we were sharing living quarters, workspaces or the grocery aisle. We learned to cough and sneeze into the crooks of our elbows, follow signs telling us which direction to push our shopping carts, and wash our hands dozens of times a day. We gathered on driveways and over Zoom to stay connected with loved ones. We celebrated healthcare workers who had become the heroes, caring for aging parents in long-term care homes and those who were terribly sick with COVID, all while putting themselves at risk.

It was a time of uncertainty and fear—fear for what lay ahead, fear of being with others lest they make us sick or we make them sick, fear of economic uncertainty and of the impacts these protocols were having on our kids.

As I reflect on that time, when we were in the most uncertain state of COVID, when there was no vaccine, I consider the impact of that time on our social cohesion, our faith in one another and our trust in government. I can see the connection between COVID and the fragile social environment we are seeing now.

I believe that people were more greatly affected by COVID than we could have imagined. Globally, we spent three years being incredibly cautious of other people. We have a generation of young people whose social skills development was seriously compromised. While we collectively managed economically through the pandemic, not everyone managed equally, and we are seeing some of those effects now.

COVID tragically took many lives, in British Columbia and around the world. There are also long-term effects—there is long COVID, but I'm talking especially about social impacts—that we may not fully comprehend for some time to come.

Overall, though, governments responded admirably with almost no blueprint for such a universal crisis. There are plenty of shortcomings to criticize, but I am proud of the way our government responded to protect all British Columbians, especially the most vulnerable.

I think voters agreed. That was the message we took when John Horgan decided to go to the polls on October 24, 2020.

## *Landslide!*

John Horgan's decision to call an election in the autumn of 2020 was controversial. We were still in the pandemic and that would make campaigning wildly different.

There was no doubt that New Democrats were in a good position to win a majority government after three-and-a-half years of the supply and confidence agreement with the Greens.

Some people accused us of taking risks and trying to gain advantage when we should still have our noses to the grindstone fighting the pandemic and its associated medical, social and economic challenges. I'm not an expert in electoral history, but I think it's safe to say that while some election campaigns begin with controversy around the calling of the election—accusations of expedience, concerns over the timing, breaking fixed election date laws—by the time people get to the polls, those details are mostly forgotten.

The bottom line, I think, is that British Columbians were happy with the government we had delivered since 2017, and that ended up being the ballot box question.

Given opinion polls saying we had a good chance at a clear victory, I felt confident in my own riding—though after the entry into provincial politics like I had in 2013, where polls said we were a shoo-in, there is a wariness that never goes away. As always, I worked my tail off campaigning.

And when I say I worked my tail off, I mean a lot of campaigning was done in dog parks. The ongoing pandemic changed everything in the campaign, as it did every aspect of life. We did some door-knocking, which is my preferred means of meeting voters, but that required knocking then backing off to a safe distance. And some people were rightly wary of a knock on the door. I chose instead to put up a sign in local parks and chat with people at a distance.

We had technology that allowed people to do telephone canvassing from home because regulations severely limited the number of people who could assemble in a campaign office.

Because of the need for social distancing, our campaign office was unlike any other, possibly in history. All four New Democrats in the Tri-Cities area jointly rented a cavernous basement in a strip mall. This was a sprawling space that ran underground for the entire length of the mall. Each campaign was located in a remote corner of this basement and, if you needed to get from one end of the place to the other, there was a bicycle you could ride. It was bizarre.

As far as province-wide campaigns go, this one was close to flawless. Having gotten to know John Horgan over more than three years as Premier, voters had come to really like him. I keep coming back to this. We ran a superb government. But likeability matters. As qualified and decent as the Liberal leader Andrew Wilkinson may have been, he just never captured the public's imagination. John ran around the province—again, limited by the pandemic restrictions—and was just John, the likeable, competent, always-upbeat guy. Next to him, Wilkinson came off as dull and somewhat grim. His patrician manner contrasted sharply with John's folksiness. Wilkinson, who is both a doctor *and* a lawyer, and whose riding included some of the province's wealthiest enclaves, did not capture the zeitgeist as voters were facing existential economic challenges.

Ultimately, the 2020 election was a test of how British Columbians felt we were managing COVID and its implications, including the economic fallout. It didn't hurt that Dr. Bonnie Henry had become a beloved figure of calm and confidence amid the most challenging medical health emergency in living memory. (Of course, in our polarized climate, she was also a lightning rod for those with beefs or conspiracy theories around the pandemic and our government's responses to it.)

Some voters didn't understand that Bonnie was a civil servant, not a New Democrat and, while we certainly did nothing to lead people to this misapprehension, I would guess most New Democrats wouldn't go out of our way to correct someone if they thought that.

Adrian Dix, as Health Minister, had proved a steady hand and another calm presence in the pandemic. Together, Adrian and Bonnie provided vital reassurance to the public all through the crisis.

Carole James, as Finance Minister, was superb in the most unimaginable, unanticipated upheaval since the Depression.

But we were popular even before our handling of the pandemic. On my file, housing, we were beginning to see some levelling off in the unaffordability crisis, although I do not pretend this macroeconomic problem was (or is) resolved.

After 16 years of BC Liberal governments that often seemed more determined to harm the most vulnerable than to help them, I think many were just happy to see people in power who demonstrated compassion. Just three-and-a-half years after ousting the entrenched Liberal government, voters didn't want to go back. We were still fresh and most people liked what they saw.

The right-wing parties—first Social Credit and then the BC Liberals—had built their successes largely on a narrative that New Democrats couldn't run an economy or balance a budget. Carole James proved them dead wrong—in the most challenging economic times imaginable. That was important. We were, above all, competent. The tired old myth that New Democrats couldn't be trusted with the purse-strings was well and truly debunked.

All's well that ends well, we say. But I have to admit to feeling really disappointed by that campaign. We won—I should hardly be complaining! But the fun and euphoria were largely stolen from us.

First of all, I love campaigning, and the way I like to do it—door to door—was largely off limits. The sense of momentum that you might expect from running a winning campaign was muted by the limited human interactions. Then there was election night. What a weird scenario.

My first provincial election, 2013, had been a massive disappointment. The NDP lost the election and I went to bed that night thinking I had lost in my riding. On election night in 2017, we were hopeful, having kept the Liberals from winning a majority, but still not sure we could oust them and form government.

The 2020 election was the night we New Democrats should have been hugging and screaming and clinking beer bottles and hollering victory from the rooftops!

Instead, we were in a cavernous basement, each of the four campaigns limited to a half-dozen immediate family and core campaign aides, masked, socially distancing and emphatically not hugging. We would shout our congratulations and happy noises at the other campaigns half a block away down the underground lair.

Of course, these minor shortcomings were eclipsed by the euphoria of finally winning a majority NDP government for the first time in 24 years.

We gained 16 seats, including a bunch in places New Democrats had never dreamed of winning. The final result was 57 New Democrats, 28 Liberals and two Greens. It was a landslide.

In the history of the province—and the almost century-long history of our party—this was only the fourth time the NDP had won a majority government. That was worth celebrating—even if we did it six feet apart.

## *Biggest challenge yet*

When John Horgan asked me to be his Minister of Finance, after the 2020 election, I had a wee bit of a freak-out. I questioned if I was ready for the task.

Finance Minister is a unique role in cabinet. Overseeing the budget and ensuring that tax dollars are spent appropriately requires oversight over all of government. That is a much greater obligation than any other portfolio save Premier.

The pressures to spend money come from all sides—inside and outside of government—and it's constant. As Finance Minister, you say no far more than yes and it's a role that doesn't necessarily win you many friends.

I had the benefit of spending my first term in cabinet as Minister of Municipal Affairs and Housing, so I was familiar with the pressures from stakeholders and others who were seeking funds to develop or deliver a much-needed initiative in their community.

As minister, you are responsible for delivering on the mandate letter that you receive from the Premier when you are first sworn in. That mandate letter becomes your work plan. And for most work plans you need money to deliver. You can only get money if the Finance Minister says you can have money. Your success in delivering for the folks who are depending on you is contingent on the Finance Minister's approval. I knew all this when John Horgan asked me to take on the portfolio.

Carole James, who was Finance Minister from 2017 until she retired in 2020, assured me that I was ready for the position. She also promised me that she wasn't far away—figuratively and literally. She lives a five-minute walk from the Legislature.

I settled into the role, working closely with the Premier and my cabinet colleagues to deliver services, programs and supports for British Columbians from all walks of life. My task was to do this while maintaining fiscal controls and a credit rating that was the envy of the country. I never in my life put in more hours at the office (even when the office was in my home during the height of the pandemic).

I have to say this: Maybe it was internalized antisemitism, but I braced myself for some commentary when I became Minister of Finance. But at no point did I ever hear anyone go to the stereotype: *They put the Jew in charge of the money*. I was waiting for it. But it never came up, even as a joke. If this convinced me that antisemitism was not going to be a problem for me, it was a bit premature.

I threw myself into my new job. Balancing the needs of various ministries, campaign commitments and personalities around the cabinet table was not easy, but I always felt supported by the Premier.

I valued that there was space and opportunity to debate and disagree within the confines of this Premier's Office. Geoff Meggs, as Chief of Staff, would often call to confirm a decision or ask a question about an opportunity. At times, I disagreed with the Premier or the Chief of Staff about a project, an analysis or a decision. There was always an openness for more discussion, an opportunity to make a case. Disagreement wasn't frowned upon or discouraged. It was seen as a chance to learn and understand concerns, or to explore the strengths and weaknesses of a project or program. And the priority was always on outcomes for people—not self-serving electoral advantage.

As I have said, I'm an optimist and a great believer in human beings. To get through potentially dark times like a global pandemic, I needed to remember human ingenuity and the things we are capable of. I had faith that people would do the right thing, keep people safe, not rip one another off, and be there for those who most needed our support. I also have faith in government to do the right thing. What saddens me right now is that people are losing faith in government. That is especially distressing because if anything should have renewed people's faith in government, it was the collective response to the pandemic. Leaving aside disagreements on approaches around vaccines and protocols, that should have been a lesson for people about the power of government to do good, just as, on a much greater scale, Franklin Roosevelt's New Deal pulled the United States back from the abyss of the Great Depression. This was a model for what government could do.

My record as Finance Minister included two surplus budgets—and given that these were "COVID budgets" that is an achievement. There were a vast number of unknowns. When you're budgeting, you project forward and the only part you really have control over is the expense part. You estimate revenues based on historical experience, economic forecasting and predictions. A once-in-a-century pandemic makes forecasting a challenge. We were extremely cautious. This proved especially fortunate, since we had yet another unexpected crisis in November of 2021 that had nothing to do with COVID. The budget planning was pretty much completed and then we had massive flooding in the Fraser Valley, a climate-related disaster that wiped out a major highway and devastated farms and valley communities.

Despite this unanticipated disaster, we had a bit more clarity about the broad economic conditions when we were drafting the 2022 budget, but again, we were still confronting COVID's impacts on healthcare expenses.

Nevertheless, we had a significant anticipated surplus—$5.7 billion—by November 2022. I'd like to say it was because of fabulous financial calculations, but really it was because of unanticipated revenue. We underestimated how strong our economy would bounce back. Overall, because we were cautious and thoughtful, we helped people get through what was a very, very difficult time.

We had a government that showed we could make the right decisions and steer the province in a way that worked for people and the health of the economy. We were also supported by a Premier who trusted his ministers to make the right decisions and supported us throughout.

The Premier, though, was pondering his own future and that would have implications for everyone in our government. The change at the top would have very specific impacts on me—and on my place in the movement and the government I had devoted myself to.

The departure of John Horgan and the selection of David Eby as our new leader and Premier, combined with world events, would ultimately lead to a rupture that shook my faith in my colleagues, my place in the party and government, and my security as a Jew in the world.

# *A Change in Leadership*

WHEN I TOLD John Horgan that I would put my name forward for re-election in 2020, I was looking forward to continuing the work that we had begun in 2017 on housing, healthcare, climate change, a just economy, and reconciliation. I knew that with John at the helm I would be supported as a colleague, friend and minister who busts her ass to get stuff done.

When John announced to cabinet in June 2022 that he would be stepping down as Premier, explaining that his cancer treatment had taken the bounce out of his step and that it was time for him to move on, I began to reflect more seriously on my own future. I began to think I too may not have the heart to run in another election in 2024.

My reflections at the time went something like this: I would be 60 years old. I would have spent 11 years as an MLA, living half the year in Victoria and travelling the province, engaging with constituents, and attending events on the weekends. As a cabinet minister, I had effectively no control over my calendar. The life of a cabinet minister is, in many ways, not your own.

My adult kids are in permanent relationships and will likely be starting their families soon. I want to be one of those bubbies who is around to help out (but mostly to spoil those children as only a *yiddishe bubbie* can).

My father and my in-laws aren't getting any younger and while I am grateful that everyone is still relatively healthy, that might not always be the case and I want to be helpful and enjoy quality time with them.

Dan was planning for retirement and aimed to start slowing down when we turned 60. I could do what I want, he'd tease me, he would send me postcards.

I never really got beyond thinking about retiring. I loved being Minister of Finance. I was good at it. With two years left before an election, I didn't really need to give re-election immediate thought.

Then the speculation began about who would fill John's shoes. Two years gives a new Premier time to make their mark, develop a brand and lead a revamped team into the next election.

I was approached many times by different people to run for leader. I felt extremely flattered. I will admit that I fantasized a bit, thinking about who I would want on my team to run a leadership campaign, what kind of campaign I would envision and, if successful, how I would lead caucus and government into the future.

While I was toying with this idea, some in the party were urging me to run "because we need a woman in the race."

## *A woman in the race?*

After all my experience across three portfolios and whatever else I might bring to leadership, my principal asset was a vagina? I would have hoped that any support I might garner would be because people thought I would be an excellent leader and Premier, that under my leadership we could deliver good things for all British Columbians—and the fact that I am a woman might be considered by some as a bonus. But if my gender was the sole reason party members wanted me to put my name forward, then I would sit this one out.

But that wasn't really the issue.

Putting my name forward for leader would commit me to run in 2024 and (if successful) again in 2028. I knew that I didn't have the energy for two more elections, let alone as party leader. Toying with the idea of running for the leadership of the BC NDP lasted about 72 hours.

Since I wasn't going to be a candidate for leader, I felt that as the Finance Minister I needed to be neutral in the contest. To run for leader, a minister needs to step away from their cabinet role. But whether they win or lose, everyone knows that this project or that initiative is "theirs." Whether the leadership candidate ascends to the premiership or returns to their previous role, the Finance Minister needs to treat all portfolios on their merits and not be seen as making decisions based on preferences in an internal party contest.

This factor was in addition to my natural avoidance of internal party fights, which can be nasty. And, as a family counsellor by training, I felt like I might have a role in bringing unity in the event that things got divisive.

When it looked like there might be a contest, David Eby called me to ask for my support. I told him I would remain neutral and explained why.

As it turned out, there really was no contest. One by one, ministers and other potential serious candidates bowed out. One far-left unelected activist entered the race and was eventually disqualified in a party decision that evoked a bit of controversy.

The party leadership race that wasn't delivered an anointment of David Eby as the new leader of the BC NDP and the 37$^{th}$ Premier of British Columbia, in November 2022.

## *A new role*

In advance of forming his first cabinet, David Eby met with caucus members to find out what their interests and plans were. A new leader routinely shuffles their cabinet to reflect their priorities and build their own team.

As Finance Minister, I was two-thirds of the way through that year's budget process, which begins annually in summer. We were near the end of the year, so a ton of work had taken place to prepare the budget for delivery in February.

When we discussed potential roles in the new cabinet, I told the new Premier I'd like to deliver the 2023 budget and then be moved to another portfolio. The timing seemed right. The 2024 budget would set the agenda for the election that fall and, although I didn't tell him this yet, I was already thinking I might not run again.

I was ready to move on—certainly from this demanding role and maybe from politics altogether. Still, I wanted to finish this budget, which was nearing completion, and then take on my next challenge. David had other ideas. But I did not expect the position he would suggest.

The Premier called me several days later as I was headed for dinner with my colleague Lisa Beare.

"I need you to be my Minister for Post-Secondary Education," he said.

It felt like a gut punch.

Post-secondary education is a portfolio that's often given to a junior minister, a first-timer, to test them out in cabinet. It's certainly not a high-profile position — or it hadn't been before.

There are 25 public post-secondary institutions in our province. The Minister of Post-Secondary Education and Future Skills is responsible for looking at institutions' funding, making sure that they have the tools they need. You hear a lot from all the college and university presidents. There's a lot of glad-handing and schmoozing.

By contrast, I had been responsible for liaising with nearly 200 local governments and all housing stakeholders in my first portfolio and overseeing the province's entire economic policy in my second. Going from finance to post-secondary is not a consistent trajectory, certainly for someone who by most measures and reports had done a good job running the province's financial affairs. The media saw it as a demotion. It's hard to argue otherwise.

In any event, if the decision was made to move me to post-sec, I was prepared to do what I always do and devote myself to it entirely.

Despite the appearance of a demotion, I am absolutely clear that serving as Minister of Post-Secondary Education was a profound privilege. I was the first in my family to graduate from university. Access to education made me the person I am. Ensuring that top-quality education, skills training and upgrading is available for British Columbians of all ages, but especially for the young, is foundational to individual and collective success.

I am not someone who believes too seriously in fate placing a person in a situation with some master plan in mind. I lean more to the idea that you are given opportunities and you make the most of them and maybe if you do well it looks like fate intervened.

Even so, when the Premier appointed me to this role, neither he nor I had any inkling that it would take on so prominent a role thanks to international events and their repercussions on BC campuses.

One of the first, very alarming things that came up on my radar was that many international students were being abused and harmed. Anecdotally, I began hearing stories, and then Kiran Singh, a reporter at CBC radio, did a story on it.

Some BC colleges, mostly private, for-profit ones, were enticing overseas students with sometimes overstated promises of the quality of education and the standards of housing they would receive. There were stories of female students having to sleep with their landlords to "pay the rent." Promises of quality accommodation might turn out to be six people in a one-bedroom apartment. These were the kinds of stories I was hearing and there was an advocacy group that was bringing these testimonies to government.

International education wasn't in my mandate letter when the Premier appointed me to this role, but as I heard more about this issue, I alerted him to it. I told him I had begun work with my civil service team to figure out the scope of this problem and find out if it is also a factor in public institutions.

BC has seen a burgeoning of both private education and the recruitment of foreign students, part of a trend across North America. There is money to be made in education, and there are plenty of people who want to come to BC from all over the world to get schooling. There is nothing inherently wrong with this situation. But for-profit businesses are first and foremost in the business of making money. Governments need to act on behalf of people, in this case students, who are, in the eyes of private colleges, "customers."

There is legislation, of course. Private colleges have to meet a minimum standard to become an institution. (The classification "university" has much more intensive requirements.) We saw an explosion of private colleges under the BC Liberals. Most of them are legitimate and their students, Canadian or not, are often happy with the education they receive and the students go on to successful lives, here or in their countries of origin.

We're not opposed to the concept of for-profit colleges, but regulations needed to be monitored and enforced. There was no auditing function when I took over the portfolio, so any enforcement was complaint-based.

Imagine you're a young woman from a village in India. Your parents and extended family have saved $40,000 a year to send you halfway around the world. You are carrying the hopes of everyone you know on your shoulders. If you complain, you could be sent home, without a degree and without the money your family had so scrupulously marshalled. Complaining was a risky proposition. Clearly, a complaints-based mechanism is inadequate in this situation.

In addition to these very serious concerns, it is notable that a lot of these schools are business colleges. They may teach useful skills, but skills are not the only thing you need to succeed in business. You need capital and you need contacts. If you come from India or Vietnam or China, you likely come with no contacts and probably no capital. If you are returning to your home country, that might be fine. But we know that many of the students who sign up are hoping to remain in Canada—and that might be a legitimate avenue for immigration if it works for both the new Canadian and for the economy here. While a business diploma can equip you with the skills you need to start or run a business, most of these students still lack the other necessities to succeed. They may end up working as baristas or as cleaners or front desk staff in hotels. These are not the types of jobs they aspired to when they made the decision to study here.

On top of these serious factors, we have a housing crisis. Foreign students make up about 30 percent of the total post-secondary population—most of these in Metro Vancouver. They often are forced into substandard housing. This is not good for them, and it adds a significant burden to the housing market.

As economies in Asia, the Pacific Rim and elsewhere elevate millions more people into the middle class, demand for educational opportunities abroad will expand significantly. BC, especially Vancouver, is a top destination. We need to be prepared to accommodate these students, ensure they receive the education they pay for and have decent housing while they are here, are not causing intolerable impacts on the broader housing market and, above all, are physically and emotionally safe.

Relatedly, there was work being done around sexual violence on campus. Rather than having every institution address this problem on their own, which was the direction they were going, I thought there could be more uniformity across the system. Yes, each of the 25 institutions has a different culture, but some of these things need to be standardized.

In addition to these major concerns around international students and sexual violence on campus, the biggest issues in the file included, of course, money. Funding is always tight. There is continuously demand for more. This is why bringing in international students is so attractive. They pay the full cost of their learning, not the taxpayer-subsidized tuition in-province students pay.

Whether students are Canadian-born or not, we need to balance the desires of individuals to pursue their dreams with the demonstrated economic needs of the province and our industry sectors. We need nurses, teachers, construction workers and so many other trained people. We need business education, too, but how much of that do we need? Institutions have academic freedom and it is a complex landscape, but we also need to balance liberal arts and other academic programs with skills training in ways that reflect the economic needs of our province as well as the interests of the students.

This is where my past experience came in handy. I have come to appreciate the value of moving people around in cabinet, allowing individuals to take things they have learned in one portfolio and bring wisdom and fresh approaches to a new file.

As post-secondary minister, I was able to partially address one of the things that had frustrated me as Minister of Finance. When I was responsible for the budget, I was pretty tough with my colleagues, who would tell me they needed more money for their portfolio. I would ask if they had the trained people to hire to do the things for which they wanted the money.

Early childhood education is a good example. We were investing significantly to build a public system of early learning, which I fully support. We were opening up childcare centres, but we were struggling to find staff because we were not training enough early childhood educators. While we need to build infrastructure, we need to simultaneously invest in training so that we have the skilled staff when the capital projects are completed. There is no point building a new hospital if there are no nurses to work there, or opening schools that lack teachers. I would tell ministers that if they couldn't demonstrate where the staffing was going to come from, they wouldn't get the funding.

As Minister of Finance, I had seen the lay of the land for all of government. I saw the gaps. In my advanced education role, I was able to ask questions of university and college leadership. I met with administrators and got to understand the economic structure of different regions of the province. I would ask whether they were talking with the major employers in their area. Were they trying to understand what the skills gaps are so they could prepare the skilled employees that their local economy needs?

Meeting the economic needs of the province was one area of focus, but we also needed to help people get access to the education they needed to build a good life. One of the things I am most proud of from my time in that role was expanding access to a life-changing program—some more tikkun olam. When the BC NDP formed government in 2017, we started providing free tuition to adults who had been children in foster care. However, that opportunity ended when people turned 27. We came to realize that those who had been in care often lacked the family and community supports many rely on—no parents' basement to return to, no quick loans from mom when rent is due, probably not a lot of mentorship from people who know their way around a college application process. As a result, they were still being left behind. We learned that many former youth in care were often not ready for post-secondary education or training because they had to find ways to just survive after they "aged out" of care at 19. We heard that in our second term and we adapted.

We removed the age limit for this support. This is a financial fix that also comes with some additional financial aid for books and equipment, but it is no silver bullet. It doesn't account for the lack of mentorship—a parent to proofread an essay, a sibling who took that course before, a general social environment where education is taken for granted—but it removed some of the most tangible economic barriers. That was exciting for me and for the thousands of people who have been in government care at some point in their lives. I had an emotional meeting with one man who was enormously impacted by the age adjustment and I saw first-hand how policy can change lives.

Unless history is deeply selective, though, none of this is what my time as Minister of Post-Secondary Education will be remembered for.

## *Decision to retire*

Once David Eby was in place as the new leader and the Legislature resumed sitting, in early 2023, the party apparatus started to gear up for the 2024 election. Incumbents were being asked to confirm their plans.

I called Premier Eby just before Christmas 2023 and told him that I had made up my mind. I wasn't going to run in the next election. The Premier expressed surprise saying, "I wasn't expecting that."

I explained that I wanted to spend more time with my family and do some of the things that I haven't had time for.

Then I added: "And caucus hasn't been the same for me since October 7."

The October 7 terror attacks and the antisemitism that swept the world after that changed everything for me, as it had for most Jewish people. By this point, I had already been through some painful interactions with colleagues and others in the party. This work is difficult enough when you feel supported as part of a team. It is much more challenging when you and your community feel under siege and the people you thought were your allies are silent—or worse.

This was the third time I had shared with the Premier that I was feeling uncomfortable in caucus, that there were undercurrents of anti-Jewish racism that were distressing for me. I was conveying to him that there was antisemitism in his government—and that this had influenced my decision to not run in the next election.

I was disappointed that he didn't ask how he could help address my discomfort in caucus. I was saddened that my distress about antisemitism did not evoke in him any greater expression of concern for me or the larger problem. On the plus side, it did assure me that my decision to leave was the right one.

At the time, however, it never crossed my mind that the decision, ultimately, would not be mine to make.

## *Bad blood?*

People have pondered whether there is bad blood between David Eby and me. If so, it doesn't come from my side. Like any colleagues in demanding jobs, we have had disagreements. To me, these seemed pretty minor.

I experienced his frustration with me in one instance over an issue involving the University Endowment Lands (UEL). As Minister of Municipal Affairs, I was the de facto mayor of the UEL, responsible for the local services in this beautiful but jurisdictionally anomalous area that includes the University of British Columbia, Pacific Spirit Park and a population of a little more than 3,000 people.

This is a small part of David's constituency of Vancouver-Point Grey and he came to me as the MLA on behalf of some constituents. They (and he) were strongly demanding that I take action to make sure that some hedges were properly trimmed (yes, actually) and we disagreed on how to best proceed. He wanted the person in charge fired. I had just come into the role and didn't think a summary firing was the way to start out. How about clarifying expectations and coming to a mutually agreeable outcome?

The hedge-trimming crisis was a minor disagreement that, because of his strong response, turned into a major conflict.

A different disagreement, one based on a misunderstanding, saw David's strong response in action again. The UEL was the source of this second quarrel as well. There was a land use process being developed to consider increased density in the area. My ministry approved the process—that is, the public engagement method through which residents and other stakeholders would have their say on the topic—but somehow David got the idea that what had been approved was the final densification decision.

I was confused, because his level of frustration over the adoption of a planning process was not commensurate with the issue. It wasn't until after he angrily hung up on me that I realized he had misunderstood what the decision meant. I sent him a text clarifying that it wasn't the final densification decision that had been made, just the process by which input for the decision would be gathered. I never heard back.

There may have been other disagreements, but we were colleagues and sometimes colleagues disagree. The idea that any of these comparatively minor incidents should have elicited serious bad blood between us is a mystery to me.

It was only after I was fired from cabinet and left the NDP caucus, in the waning days of my time as MLA, that I learned something absolutely dumbfounding.

I have heard from more than one source that, around the time I was appointed Finance Minister, David called other ministers trying to corral them to demand that Premier Horgan reconsider appointing me to the role. Never in my experience in politics or even in my reading of history have I heard of a colleague mobilizing a campaign to pressure a head of government to influence the appointment of a member of cabinet they didn't like.

Given that David Eby apparently tried to launch a cabinet revolt to prevent me from becoming Finance Minister, it is no surprise in retrospect that he shuffled me out of there at the first opportunity when he became Premier.

To be fair, he likely knew from experience that I would stand up to him and maybe that wasn't what he was looking for in a Finance Minister.

Given the comparatively insignificant (to me and probably to most reasonable observers) nature of our past disagreements, David's apparent dislike baffles me. It will be up to someone else to ask him what he has against me, but the evidence is there to suggest something about me sets him off.

One additional incident that told quite a bit about David Eby's style was his firing of the entire Board of Directors of BC Housing after he succeeded me as Minister of Housing.

BC Housing is the Crown agency where the government's rubber hits the road on one of the most important issues we face. As Housing Minister, it is on your agenda every morning.

In 2022, an Ernst & Young review of the agency found inadequate oversight around some spending and other decisions, as well as unclear roles and responsibilities the report said could limit the agency's ability to manage risks.

Late on a Friday, David dropped a press release announcing that he had fired the entire board. It surprised everyone, including me. As his predecessor in this portfolio, I had originally vetted the board members, who are ultimately appointed by cabinet. Many of them were then re-appointed by David. There was no explanation offered and these members, individuals with stellar academic and community reputations, now had to stave off suspicion of wrongdoing—even though David went so far as to publicly assure that they had done nothing wrong.

In the absence of an explanation, outside observers often go to the worst-case scenario. These were good people, experts in their various fields, who were volunteering their time. Their reputations were tarnished because David chose not to provide enough detail or context on the firing.

The Ernst & Young report identified some issues that required addressing and the minister's reaction seemed the most severe imaginable. It appeared to me that his need was to make the problem go away instantly, rather than deal with it in an appropriate, mature manner. At a moment of serious crisis in an organization, an experienced board is more essential than ever. They could have been given the opportunity to remedy the problems. Instead, all of that institutional memory was flushed in one swift move.

David Eby seems to like making big, bold moves. But they can create bigger problems. I think what he was trying to do in this instance was to be seen as decisive.

He was gunning for the party leadership by this point and perhaps he wanted to be seen as someone who takes strong actions in crucial moments. From my perspective, this kind of decisiveness ends up seeming more like a bull in a china shop.

You might want to do that in a campaign, but that's not how you should govern. He was campaigning for the job of Premier. We were trying to govern.

Then there are some behaviours that are less substantive, but that pull back the curtain to suggest a leadership style. Small actions or oversights can be deeply telling about a person's character.

At the BC NDP convention in November 2023—where I was publicly targeted by the protesters who would eventually bring me down—the Premier, of course, made a keynote speech to the 1,000 or so assembled delegates.

This was his first convention as party leader and would be the only such meetup before the election scheduled for 11 months later. All the MLAs were gathered together to march into the convention hall before the Premier gave his address. The Premier's wife, Dr. Cailey Lynch, took the microphone to introduce him. The 50+ MLAs stood on the stage behind the Premier's podium, providing a solid backdrop of support as the leader made his way to the stage, his kids in tow and rightly basking in the ovation of an excited crowd of invigorated New Democrats.

The Premier talked about the achievements we had made as a government and the work we needed to keep doing under renewed leadership to make life better for British Columbians. It was the typical rah-rah rallying cry delegates expect from their leader at these rare events.

Except, not once during his speech did this leader refer to any of the more than four dozen individuals standing behind him. When he addressed a policy area, he gave no credit to the relevant minister. He gave no indication whatsoever that the human props behind him had played any part in our success as a government.

Then there was something deeply personal that still leaves me mystified as a colleague and as a human being.

In February 2023, I announced that my cancer had returned. I told the Premier that I would mention it in my remarks during the upcoming Throne Speech debate. I assured him that the return of the cancer would not inhibit my ability to do my job.

By October, the cancer had disappeared. In all that time, the Premier never once asked for an update or asked me how I was doing. It seems so odd. Given the multitude of opportunities he had over the better part of a year, before or after scores of meetings, or through a text or phone call, I cannot imagine being in a situation like that and not inquiring about a colleague's health when they have very publicly acknowledged cancer.

In contrast, I was talking to an opposition MLA whose daughter had required a very dangerous surgery a few years ago. He told me how John Horgan called the MLA to ask about his daughter soon after her surgery—recognizing the fear and worry this father felt about his daughter's well-being.

I was dealing with a caucus where I did not feel my colleagues would have my back and who seemed incapable of empathizing with my position as a Jew in the post-October 7 reality while navigating as part of a government that was growing increasingly alienated from my community of people.

I cannot express how sapping it was, on top of this, to work with a Premier who knew I was living with cancer for eight months and never once asked how I was doing. He was the Premier of the province, a busy guy. I get that. But when one of your cabinet ministers has a life-threatening condition, and you know you are not the kind of person who is likely to remember or demonstrate natural concern, it is almost worth asking an assistant to put it in your calendar every few months. "Ask Selina how cancer treatment is going."

All of these factors added up to reassure me I had made the right decision in telling the Premier I would not be seeking re-election.

Within weeks, the pleasant idea that I had control over my political future would seem woefully misguided.

# *The Interregnum*

IN MANY WAYS, getting the phone call from the Premier telling me that he didn't "see a way forward" was not so much the end of something, but the beginning of something new. It is fridge magnet wisdom that when one door closes another opens. But of course it's true.

My ouster from cabinet—I call it a firing, the Premier calls it a resignation, the press release called it a joint decision—began a month-long period of what my Yiddish-speaking great-grandparents would have called *nisht ahin un nisht aher*, neither here nor there. Eventually, I would use a Latin term for this period: the interregnum.

After the news release went out announcing I was no longer in cabinet, in the early afternoon of February 5, my phone wouldn't stop. People were calling and texting. Some were sympathetic, others were disappointed. I was totally spent and crawled into bed for a much-needed sleep.

While I snoozed, the Premier was speaking to media.

"The reason for this decision is that, over the past few days, both Minister Robinson and myself have been reaching out to the many communities that have been harmed by her remarks made on a panel that she participated in, to understand how to make things better," he said. "When you hurt somebody, you need to reach out to them and try to figure out what the best way is to reduce the harm and address the hurt that has been caused. The depth of the work that Minister Robinson needs to do in order to address the harms that she's caused is significant and it is incompatible with her continuing as Minister of Advanced Education, given the volume and the depth of the work that she needs to do. It's certainly a challenging decision for Selina, for me, that she will take this step, but it is important to recognize that the harm and the hurt in communities is the focus here. We have a lot of work to do as government, British Columbians are facing big challenges, and we need to be there for them and we need to be bringing people together. So Selina's work for the next little while will be focusing on addressing that division that she increased with those comments."

When I awoke, I was greeted by a desperate text message from the Premier's Chief of Staff, Matt Smith, at 2:08 PM: "Please give me a call." Then at 2:16: "Selina someone is talking to media with lies and I want to touch base w you on it." At 2:45: "Selina it is urgent. We need to respond to [Vancouver Sun reporter] Katie DeRosa saying the Premier forced you out. As you know you said to Premier 'if you want my resignation, I will give it.'"

"Just woke from a nap," I replied. "My recollection is Premier called me telling me that caucus wants me to resign. He didn't see a path forward and he believed I needed to resign. My response was I won't fight you on it. I am not happy about that. I offered to accept the will of caucus and the Premier."

I followed up with a call telling him that I suspect Katie figured out the difference between the Premier's changing position of defending me on Friday and announcing a "joint decision" to resign on Monday. I also pointed out that because the Premier wanted my resignation, I was forced out, so Katie had simply ferreted out the truth.

In any event, it was the Premier's problem now.

My mind turned to what's next.

I had not yet talked to my ministry staff or my community office team, and I felt responsible for helping them understand what this would mean for them. There was so much to do, but the nap barely assuaged my exhaustion.

I made a few unavoidable phone calls and then turned to Dan.

"I need to get out of here," I said. I suggested we find a holiday package to Mexico and that we bring our kids and their partners.

I needed a distraction from everything that was swirling around me. I knew that my daughter Leya and her partner Omer would likely be able to join us. They both work in the Jewish community and their respective bosses would want to support my family. Having my kids around would help me focus on what was important. My son Aaron and his husband Kyle weren't able to make it, unfortunately, so Dan got busy on the internet trying to find a quick getaway for four.

About then, several of my erstwhile cadre of female colleagues showed up at my front door. When I saw Lisa Beare among them, the "friend" whose phone call hours earlier at the height of my crisis struck me as such a betrayal, my emotions rose.

Her words came back to me in a rush—her urging me to fall on my sword with the ridiculous fantasy that there could be an opportunity for me to return to cabinet when things died down. I had no interest in drinking their wine. I thanked them for the thought and turned them away.

As they walked down the driveway, Mike Farnworth and Rob Fleming showed up. I laugh thinking what the two groups might have said to one another. The women might have warned the men that Selina was in a foul mood and they'd best reverse course. But I warmly welcomed Mike and Rob (and the bottle of scotch they brought along). Along with Murray Rankin, Rob and

Mike were the only New Democrat colleagues who seemed to have any appreciation for what I was going through. Consistently, they had checked in with me as antisemitism exploded, they were the only ones who expressed empathy around the succession of indignities and betrayals I had gone through.

We sat drinking scotch, talking about what had happened and where we were heading as a society. My next-door neighbour Peter showed up with enough Indian food to feed the block. I was grateful for the company, for a neighbour who knew that we needed to eat, for a husband who moved into action and booked us a getaway to Mexico, and for two colleagues who understood what was at stake.

The next 48 hours are a bit of a blur—and not because of the scotch. Dan and I packed a few things and prepared to disappear to Mexico. I guess that occupied my time because I can't honestly recall how I spent Tuesday, the first day in six years that I was free from the 24/7 obligations of a provincial cabinet minister.

On Wednesday morning, February 7, I discovered that there were people for whom my resignation was not enough. My staff arrived at our community office and discovered it had been vandalized with ugly, antisemitic messages. There were scores of photographs, images and comments stuck to my windows and doors. It was quite a lot of effort to go to.

I was no longer in cabinet. I had been forced to resign because the mob demanded it, and yet it still wasn't enough. What did they want? What would satiate their rage?

The next day, Thursday, I was sitting next to Dan on the plane, preparing to take off for Mexico. In the seconds before I turned off my phone, I received a call from Iti Kalsi, my Constituency Assistant.

My community office team were still ploughing through the hundreds of emails that had been flooding in, almost none of which were from constituents or had anything to do with the responsibilities of an MLA. They were mostly from people outside of Coquitlam who had decided that I was either an evil Jew who got what she deserved or folks who offered support, acknowledging that while my choice of words was inelegant, I said nothing harmful and had nothing to apologize for.

But then they came across a death threat. There are very particular protocols in place for these situations. My staff immediately notified Legislature security and the RCMP, then called me.

Unfortunately, as a woman politician I already had experience with death threats. My community office had previously received a series of ugly misogynistic emails from an individual who promised very specific violence. In that situation, the response had seemed somewhat haphazard, but security and the police learned something from that and (as I discovered later) other threats from the same deeply troubled person. The response in this instance was much more streamlined.

I was so grateful that I had decided to get out of town for a bit. I would not have been comfortable at home. I directed my staff to not work out of the office. I also asked them to let our landlord know of the threat so that the other tenants in the building would be aware that the situation might create some risk for those who shared my workspace.

I wasn't particularly frightened for me. I was angrier and more frustrated for my staff who were on the frontlines of receiving this hostility, and now had to incorporate additional safety protocols into their workday. I was angry because those who shared my office building were potentially endangered. I was angry because my husband felt it was now necessary to keep a baseball bat in our bedroom. I was angry that my children now had to worry for my safety. I was angry because the Premier and my colleagues either didn't know or didn't care how bad antisemitism had become. And I was angry because the leaders of the party and the government, of which I was still nominally a part, were more worried about votes than about doing the right thing.

Our week in Mexico, although distracting, wasn't fun or even relaxing. Sleep was still mostly elusive as my mind kept playing numerous scenarios over and over. Why did I say, "crappy piece of land"? What if I had just said "Young people don't understand the history of Jews, the impact of the Holocaust and the founding of the modern State of Israel"? What if I had stood firm and told the Premier that I simply would not resign? What if I told him that he needs to own the fact that he didn't like the noise being made by these anti-Israel activists and that my apology should suffice?

I also contemplated the future. I couldn't change the past, but could I make something good come from it? I have always been a forward-looking person and I've always focused on what was possible. If I created damage in some way, I needed to repair it.

This is very much a Jewish concept called *t'shuvah*—literally meaning "return," but practically translated as "repentance." The teaching is that, if you do wrong, you take responsibility for it, you learn from it, you make amends with the affronted person or group, if possible, and you commit to not repeat the transgression. Ideally, you find some action that improves the situation, even if you cannot undo the original offence.

Resigning from cabinet would leave me with fewer responsibilities. Being an MLA is hard work but, compared to the hectic schedule of a minister, my changed circumstance would leave me with time and energy to take on a new project.

I had become an MLA with the aim of doing good in the world. If I could use the role that I have and the relationships that I have made to address people who are hurting, then I could continue to do meaningful work.

As part of my t'shuvah, the Premier asked that I make a series of calls to Muslim community leaders. I began to think: What if I could engage with these groups and bring the Jewish community and the Arab and Muslim communities together in some way? These two heartbroken communities, both fearful for their families overseas and feeling powerless to effect change, could find commonality in that shared experience, at the very least. Action is always an antidote to hopelessness and helplessness. I could do this as part of my role as an MLA and the government could take credit for doing something meaningful that makes a positive difference for both these aching communities. For me, this would be a profound form of redemption, of t'shuvah, and also of tikkun olam.

I reached out to Deborah Lyons, Canada's Special Envoy for Holocaust Remembrance and Combatting Antisemitism, to see what she thought of the idea. I thought I could engage her and Amira Elghawaby, Canada's Special Representative on Combatting Islamophobia, in this work. I thought maybe the Premier would provide me with a staff person from the public service, perhaps a Muslim person who could be my partner in a project of engaging our respective communities. As part of the work, caucus could do training around both antisemitism and Islamophobia. I began to dream bigger. This could be a model for the rest of Canada, maybe for Legislatures in other countries. We could forge a positive new path, demonstrating leadership on this vexing and divisive issue.

Deborah was enthusiastic.

This was the first ray of hope I had felt in a very long time.

I contacted the Premier while I was still in Mexico to talk with him about the idea. I told him that I already had support in principle from the Special Envoy, who had offered to help in any way she could. We chatted briefly as I laid out what it could look like. He said it was an interesting concept and that we should talk more about it when I got back.

I looked forward to returning home and hashing out these ideas a bit more. From my despair, I was beginning to feel a sense of returning hope.

* * *

I knew that first week back at the Legislature would be tough, but I massively underestimated just how painful it would be.

Emotionally, I was so hurt that I really did not want to be there. The Premier and his Chief of Staff had told me to take all the time I needed. Perhaps they would have preferred if I never came back.

In beautiful Victoria, which I had come to love in my 11 years there, it felt like the entire city was staring at me. It is hard to know whether this was all in my head or whether judgment did indeed follow me around. I had stopped tracking the news, so I didn't know if my face was still everywhere. I didn't know what people thought amid all this. Did they genuinely believe I was an Islamophobe, a racist, a heartless monster who didn't care about Palestinians?

I felt utterly alone, able to trust no one.

But I had a job to do, and I was committed to doing it. I would hold my head high and get to work.

I received a text message from Matt Smith the day before the session started.

"Hi Selina, checking in. You are in Victoria this week and I wanted to see if you need support around anything."

I responded the following morning by text.

"At this point not sure what that would look like.

"I don't have an office to go to when I arrive and Garry [Begg, MLA for Surrey-Guildford and Party Whip] only said that all will be good so not sure what that means.

"I understand that there is likely to be a protest at the Legislature and given a death threat and anti-Jewish sentiment right now it doesn't feel particularly safe for me."

In response to this expression of vulnerability, I heard nothing.

I eventually heard from Garry that they had an office space for me located in the East Annex, where most of the NDP back-benchers had their offices. I would be sharing a space with these folks and the specific office that I was given faced directly to the front of the Legislature lawns. It's usually a beautiful view. But on the first day of the session, featuring the Speech from the Throne, it was swarming with dozens of people, faces covered with keffiyehs, chanting "From the river to the sea, Palestine will be free." They carried signs accusing Zionists of being genocidal killers and other hateful messages. This is what greeted me as I arrived in my new office and this is what I listened to all day long. Their chants were endless, and I had nowhere else to go. I had to be in the building as all of caucus was supposed to be there. I suppose I could have asked for leave and just gone home, but that would have been an admission of defeat.

I had interesting interactions with two different industry sector people who were invited to hear the speech that day. Both are Jewish women who wanted to see me. Both these women shared similar stories. They felt intimidated and harassed by the protesters as they made their way into the building. One felt she needed to hide the Star of David that she wore around her neck and had asked for a security escort into the building. The other was just appalled that these people could spew such hatred at Jews—words and images that would not be tolerated were they directed toward any other community. I was inclined to agree with both their assessments. It was shameful behaviour that was being tolerated by our institutions and by our government. We were struggling to see the line between "free speech" and "hate speech." We wondered how far a group would be permitted to go before it was deemed inappropriate and illegal.

Meanwhile, none of my ostensible colleagues came to see how I was doing. No one seemed to notice that the hatred raging outside my window was directed at me. No one mentioned the death threat and the effect that had on my well-being and that of my family.

That was probably the most difficult day I had ever had in the Legislature. And I have had plenty of difficult days. I have delivered two budgets, been on my feet for hours at a time answering question after question from the opposition, I have had to face tough media interrogations. But all of that pales in comparison with what it was like to sit in that little office, with little to do except listen to the hatred directed toward me, my family and my people.

The following days and weeks were a little easier. The idea of a Jewish-Muslim dialogue of some form, which I came to think of as "The Project," was the light at the end of a dark tunnel. I was eager to see if the Premier would approve my proposal, hoping that it could help bring people together at a time when our communities were being torn apart. From my darkness, this was the ray of light. I knew that my career in politics was nearing an end—it had been my choice to not seek re-election, but I had expected to spend my last few months as a constructive, engaged cabinet minister. Now, adrift and bereft, the idea that I could turn this terrible experience into something positive was a redemptive passion. It was a chance for a last important act of tikkun olam that would allow me to end my time in office on a hopeful, positive note.

Matt Smith asked to meet with me so I could share with him the framework I was thinking about. He took notes and said he would get back to me.

I waited two weeks. In the interim, I made calls to Muslim leaders, with some limited success.

I attended caucus meetings as required, sitting in the back of the room, barely engaging with anyone.

In the Legislative Chamber, I sat in my new seat at the far end of the House. It was a different experience to be in Question Period without having the familiar adrenaline rush that comes with the possibility that you might be asked a question by an opposition member.

I went through the motions as a caucus member but that was all I was doing. I clapped when it seemed appropriate, but my heart wasn't in it. I was so hurt and saddened by what had transpired, but I hung on to the idea that I could at least be doing something meaningful that would help heal the Arab, Muslim and Jewish communities.

At the end of the second week of the session, Matt Smith asked to meet with me again.

I hoped he would tell me the Premier was interested in my project. Instead, he told me that the project I had proposed was "too political" and that it would be impossible to use ministry resources to make it happen. It was a 10-minute meeting that took away what little hope I had remaining.

It felt like a switch went off. After all that had happened, it felt like the Premier was taking away even this, my eleventh-hour effort at repairing the world in what small way I might. I was absolutely done.

I knew in that moment that this was no longer my place, no longer my government, no longer my political party. A place and a party where I belonged would recognize the opportunity for someone who was seen to have transgressed to do some good. My place, my party, would recognize the value of bringing people together. A place where I belonged would not be afraid to try something unique and potentially powerful.

I went home to Coquitlam that Thursday night and started drafting what I intended to be a speech that I would make at the caucus meeting the following week, a speech that would explain why I could no longer be part of a New Democrat team that time after time had betrayed me and refused to do the right thing.

That speech turned into a letter, a heartfelt missive that explained why I was quitting the New Democrat caucus.

When I returned to the Legislature the following Monday, I was unsure about when or how to deliver the letter. I wanted to face caucus and read the letter, but it was much too long, and I didn't think I could get the time to say what I needed to say.

I was also hesitant. Delivering this letter would create another upheaval, more media attention, more emotional chaos. It would mean my community office would be cut off from all caucus supports. My small staff of two would be utterly alone to deal with the vast range of inquiries and requests for assistance that every MLA receives.

As an MLA, I would really be on my own.

I reasoned that I was on my own anyway. I wasn't getting the support I needed and hadn't been for some months. I had been pleading into an abyss that the atmosphere for Jews was deteriorating and no one in the government seemed willing to address it. They would wring their hands, insisting that antisemitism was not OK. But they weren't doing anything. A government that prided itself on taking bold action in support of marginalized communities was not taking bold action. They were not taking any action. If they didn't know how to respond, I was right there to advise them. I had been pleading, offering specific steps, urging solidarity. But, not only were my colleagues not coming to ask me how they should respond, they were turning away when I asked them to take a stand. There wasn't much more alone I could get.

That day, as I was walking down the vacant Speaker's corridor behind the House, out of sight from the public, I bumped into Vaughn Palmer who can frequently be seen pacing the back hallways of the Legislature, looking for fodder for his *Vancouver*

*Sun* column. He asked how I was. "As well as can be expected," I replied. He then leaned in and said, "What happened to you was wrong." The heaviness in my heart lifted a bit. He followed up with "What happened to you was not fair." I stopped, turned to Vaughn and thanked him for his words. I told him, "This means more to me than you can ever know." In that moment, I knew that it was time to act on that letter.

No sooner had I made the decision to release my resignation letter than I received word that the Premier wanted to meet with me in two days, on Wednesday, March 6, which happened to be my 60th birthday.

I postponed releasing my letter. I had no idea why the Premier wanted to meet. Though I didn't anticipate a birthday cake, I was hopeful. Maybe he had reconsidered my project. Maybe, just maybe, there was a way forward, a way that I could be a part of something that made a difference. Something that could do a small bit to confront the division that had landed on our shores.

I arrived at the Premier's Office a little early. I was eager to hear what he wanted. He asked how I was doing. "OK, given the circumstances," I replied.

Then he asked me how things were with my colleagues. I shrugged and was noncommittal because, in my mind, I was already leaving. I also wondered why he would care now. It had been a month since I was kicked out of cabinet. I had not heard a word from him in that time. We'd had no interactions whatsoever. Now, it felt like he was asking the questions because he had to, not because he cared. It felt like the absolute minimum he could do before moving on to what I believe was the real purpose of our meeting.

He asked if I knew that my constituency executive, the Coquitlam-Maillardville BC NDP volunteers who help with election preparation and maintain the party apparatus between campaigns, was planning to write a letter to the party expressing discontent with my treatment. I told him I was aware that they were unhappy.

Then he asked my thoughts about him reaching out to them to encourage them not to write the letter as it would only cause more grief. I told the Premier that he could talk to anyone he wants. I was fine with him communicating directly with my executive.

That was it. Now I understood why he called me to his office. It wasn't to check on how I was, either physically or emotionally. He certainly wasn't overriding his Chief of Staff's veto of my project.

It appeared to me that the real reason he invited me to meet him was to see if I would shut down my executive before they publicly criticized him.

I made my way back to my office, turned on my computer and hit send. And with that, I ceased to be a member of the New Democratic caucus.

## *Letter to my colleagues*

> My colleagues,
>
> You broke my heart—not just on February 5 when the Premier told me that after the caucus talked about me he did not see a way back, that folks were wondering why I hadn't already resigned and that the only path forward was a resignation. Resigning was not my choice but I told the Premier that if this was what he wanted and what caucus wanted I wouldn't fight him on it—but let's be clear—others asked for my resignation, so I gave it.
>
> You actually broke my heart in the days after October 7—the day terrorists went into Israel and

brutally murdered, slaughtered, raped, mutilated, killed and kidnapped 1,200 civilians. These terrorists didn't target the military, they killed children, concert-goers, grandmothers, peace activists and a young British Columbian named Ben Mizrachi.

The Jewish community was in shock—we are about 40,000 here in British Columbia and we were reeling.

I had offered to the Premier that, as a member of the Jewish community, I could speak at a vigil that was being planned a few days after the massacre—this was my community and our two Premiers had tasked me with strengthening the NDP relationship with the community. I put out the call for you to join me. The community was grieving, in mourning, and we needed to show them as a caucus and as a government that we are there for them.

I sent out a group email. Two, maybe three, responded—that's it. How is it that with more than 35 Lower Mainland/Valley MLAs, only three or four would be on stage with me? I had no idea how many [opposition members] would be there and a poor showing would not reflect well on us. I did not have the emotional capacity to reach out individually, so Alissa offered to help . . . still not much response. My heart cracked.

In the end, there were 7 or 8 of us, two came from the island, but I was terribly embarrassed.

And then, within days of the massacre, Aman and Katrina decided that it was appropriate to "reply all" to my initial email asking folks to stand with the Jewish community in grief and mourning, and ask that government make a public statement about the plight of the Palestinians.

We just witnessed the slaughter, rape, mutilation and murder of 1,200 mostly Jews. We watched as the terrorists celebrated this horrific act. Ben Mizrachi hadn't yet been buried. The IDF hadn't yet taken any action. The world was stunned. And two of my colleagues wanted to move quickly past what had happened and refocus government on a geopolitical conflict that has been going on for years.

But it wasn't their antisemitism that broke my heart. It was your silence to their antisemitism that hurt the most. Not a single one of you responded to their insensitive, disrespectful and inappropriate email. No one.

Your silence broke my heart that day.

You abandoned me and my community that day.

I would have hoped that someone, anyone, would have replied all to Aman and Katrina and suggested that their email was inappropriate—your silence spoke volumes to me and suggested that either you agreed with them or that you just didn't want to deal with it because it's messy.

It is messy. It's complex. It's emotional. It's hard. You just want it to go away. I understand. I want it to go away too—but my community needed you in that moment to be there in their grief and in my grief and none of you were prepared or willing to stand up to colleagues who were antisemitic—minimizing the Jewish experience, the slaughter of innocent civilians by terrorists countering with mirrored message about the plight of Palestinians. In that moment, it was not so complex. People were murdered because they were Jewish and people here in British Columbia were needing us to mourn with them.

How eager you all are to join in the #NeverAgain campaign—that the crime of being Jewish that resulted in the death of six million Jews at the hands of the Nazis should never happen again. That we should fight against

Jew-hatred—a hatred that repeats itself over and over and over again throughout history. How eager you all are to join the few remaining Holocaust survivors as Nicholas plays Kol Nidre on the cello and we bow our heads, light candles in honour of those murdered. Yet when the hordes gather and chant "From the river to the sea"—a Hamas mantra referring to their desire to destroy Israel and the Jews—you are nowhere to be found.

Holocaust survivors have been retraumatized and some have wound up in hospital in the days and weeks after the massacre as they relive the horrors they experienced some 75 years ago. They see the marches, the chanting in our streets, the threats to Jews around the world and they say, "It's happening again."

Where are you when protesters, their faces covered, march through our campuses intimidating young Jewish adults who now hide their Jewish identity? Where are you when young Jewish students get trapped in bathrooms on campus because the marching is happening in hallways, and they are afraid to step out into the hall for fear of becoming a target of their hate? Where are your ideals of a broad, inclusive society? How have you been standing up for your declared values?

Almost 300 Jewish physicians signed a letter calling on UBC medical school to address antisemitism on campus. Students are bringing their hate into healthcare and they were speaking on behalf of their Jewish patients and their families. In fact, it was so bad that Ted Rosenberg, a prominent physician, quit, citing a toxic work environment and antisemitism in the Faculty of Medicine—I am not sure how we expect to train more physicians when almost 300 of them are refusing to work with students coming from UBC's Faculty of Medicine. It was a public leaving and I heard nothing from any of you—not the Minister of Health who committed to more physicians in the system, not the Premier—no one.

In December, the four Tri-Cities MLAs received a letter from the Coquitlam Teachers Association rife with rhetoric, misinformation and lies about the modern State of Israel. The letter was also posted on their website (which has since been taken down). Jewish parents in SD 43 are now considering pulling their children from public schools because they don't have faith that teachers in the district will keep their Jewish children safe. I asked Fin if he received the same letter. He did, and when I asked him what he was planning to do with it he said, "Nothing—I am going to ignore it." Ignore the fact that Jewish constituents feel unsafe? Is this how we stand up for our constituents?

In January, the Vancouver Police Department publicly shared a startling report about the dramatic increase in antisemitic incidents since October 7. And what was government's response to this report?

Silence.

Shortly afterward, I reached out to the Attorney General as the racism file is under her ministry. Niki had been assigned the point of contact for the Jewish community because of the antisemitism that the Jewish community has experienced from Mable Elmore, the Parliamentary Secretary for Antiracism.

So I reached out to Niki at the end of January, two months after she became the designated point of contact for a community that is experiencing a spike in antisemitism, a community that is grieving and fearful. It turns out that the community leadership hadn't even heard from her. And when I asked her what she is doing about the rise in antisemitism all she could talk about [was] what legislation she is working on, collecting data and the small amount of money that I worked on with [Public Safety and Solicitor General] and the [Premier's Office] to make available for additional security measures that the community needed.

Her response to my query was a response you would give the opposition.

There was no acknowledgement of my personal connection to the community or how my contacts and relationships could be useful. There was no sense of understanding that this community is feeling threatened, that people are afraid, that antisemitism was on display in civil society, that Jewish parents don't want to send their children to public school, that Jewish post-secondary students are being terrorized on campus, that Jewish-owned businesses need additional security, that Holocaust survivors are reliving trauma, that plays with Israeli content that actually help to provide dialogue about the conflict are being silenced, that hundreds of Jewish physicians are calling on UBC leadership to address antisemitism on campus, that members of our own public service have started incorporating the Palestinian flag in their email signature and even making a Palestinian land comment when doing a First Nations land acknowledgement at the beginning of meetings, resulting in discomfort and fear. No acknowledgment and no action.

Over the past five months, a few of you have reached out after caucus discussions about me without me in the room, the first right after Aman and Katrina sent their emails and then again after the February caucus meeting, offering hugs and heart emojis. My response to many of you is that I don't need your hugs and your emojis. What my community needs however is for you to stand up to antisemitism. When I shared this with Lisa just a few weeks ago, she responded "Of course, we always do." As a government, we have not been standing up to antisemitism. If you believe that [we are], then it would appear to me that you haven't been paying attention or you don't know what antisemitism is or what Jew-hatred looks like.

Antisemitism is calling for the destruction and annihilation of Israel where half the world's 15.8 million Jews live. Antisemitism is making Jewish people afraid to show their identity. Antisemitism is silencing an openly identified Jewish person who is speaking out about antisemitism. Your collective decision to silence me is antisemitism and you don't even know it.

Antisemitism is the double standard that we have consistently shown. When any of my colleagues have made antisemitic remarks, it was expected that apologies should suffice. It's not only Mable who has made antisemitic comments. In 2012, Jennifer Whiteside shared content from the anti-Israel website the Electronic Intifada and posts from Occupy Wall Street that attributed Israeli "theft" of Palestinian land to capitalism and, in 2014, shared articles that accused Israel of "pinkwashing" for their acceptance of LGBTQ2S+ community and again, in 2016, shared content promoting the BDS movement and was forced to apologize and distance herself from her past support of the BDS movement.

In 2017, it came to the attention of the Jewish community that Ronna-Rae invited people to support Haneen Zoubi, a former Palestinian member of the Israeli Knesset who negated the existence of Israel. Ronna-Rae also compared the police to Nazis in 2013.

Jagrup quoted Goebbels in 2020 when he was pushing back at the official opposition during a speech in the House, saying, "Someone has said—if you repeat a lie often enough people will believe it." He apologized the next day for his offence, retracted his comments and that was to be sufficient.

Last year, Janet Routledge apologized for comments of Holocaust minimization by comparing the criticisms by the official opposition to Nazi rhetoric when she said, "The Holocaust ended in death camps, but started with words."

I raise these examples not to humiliate or shame any of you, but to point out the double standard. When an elected person says something that harms the Jewish community, whether the comments or position are intended or unintended, the expectation is that a simple apology is sufficient. But when a Jewish elected person says something, she "has deep work to do," according to the Premier, and is no longer trusted. This double standard is antisemitism.

The final straw came for me last week.

I pitched an idea to the Premier 10 days after I was asked to resign that perhaps government could show leadership on this hate and division we are seeing in two hurting communities by bringing these communities together. I suggested that perhaps I could work with the Jewish community and engage with the Arab Muslim community to facilitate dialogue—find a different path for two communities in agony. As part of that work, all of caucus could participate in anti-Islamophobia and antisemitism training—set an example of how as leaders we could better understand their respective pain and fear. And government could show leadership by bringing people together.

Last week, Matt Smith told me that this work was "too political" and that government was not interested at this time. Antisemitism and anti-Muslim sentiment are at an all-time high and government doesn't see itself as having a role in helping these communities.

This shattered what was left of my broken heart.

This is not the party I signed on with—it has become a party that is afraid to stand with people, people who are hurting. It is now a party that puts politics and re-election before people.

It is with all of this in mind that I am leaving caucus to sit as an independent. I can no longer defend the choices this government is making, and I need to mend my broken heart and I can't do that when you simply offer me hugs and heart emojis but don't care to educate yourselves or understand the fear and anguish of being Jewish in this moment.

Silence is not leadership—it's cowardice.

And I cannot be silent.

* * *

I would spend my last weeks as an MLA on the opposition side of the House—where my time in the Legislature had begun. It was a sort of full circle, albeit not as I would have planned it.

From this perch, I would hold the government to account on issues that remained important to me and to the Jewish community. I made what I think are important interventions on legislation to protect British Columbians, especially children, from racism and discrimination. I would pursue tikkun olam in my own way, freed from the fetters of party politics, until the clock ran out on my years in elected office.

But that relatively calm denouement to my career in government was still in the future. First, I had to get through the blowback I knew my letter would elicit.

I had my say. Then others had theirs.

"As a leader, for me, it's a real day for examination of what the opportunities were, where I could have potentially intervened and addressed some of the concerns Selina had," the Premier told CBC when asked about my resignation. "I had a meeting with her just a few hours before she resigned from our caucus. I was checking in with her. How are you doing? How is your relationship with colleagues? How is the community feeling? How's your work going with the Muslim community? And she didn't feel safe raising these issues with me. So, for me, that's a message that I need to examine, how I work with our team, because Selina's voice was an important one in our caucus. She had an experience of the October 7 attack attacks that nobody else in our caucus had."

I noticed he went out of his way to share with the public a litany of questions he posed to me, but he didn't share what appeared to me to be the actual reason for the meeting. He called me to his office because he was worried that my constituency executive was writing a mean letter about him.

He was correct on this: He didn't create a space to find out how I was really feeling, even when I opened the door for us to discuss how I was feeling on multiple occasions. I had told him that Aman's response to my email was hurtful. I had told him that the NDP convention was hard for me given resolutions that I considered antisemitic. When I shared with him that I would not be seeing re-election, I told him that caucus had changed for me. He never really demonstrated any concern for my well-being—emotionally, as I was going through a period of profound anguish, or physically, since I had been dealing with cancer for most of the past year and he had never once inquired how that was going.

The Premier's words to the media after I released my letter were curious for another reason. When he fired me, the Premier told the world that I couldn't continue as a cabinet minister because of the "depth of the work" I had to do—work that had only the remotest connection, if any, to my actual responsibilities.

Now, here he was again telling media that someone had work to do—this time, himself. "It's a real day for examination of what the opportunities were, where I could have potentially intervened and addressed some of the concerns Selina had. . . . That's a message that I need to examine, how I work with our team."

Indeed. That's some deep work. I think it goes directly to the heart of his role as a leader, something that speaks to the very specific capacities he needs to do his job. But clearly, unlike my deep work, the Premier seemed to conclude that this was something he could do off the side of his desk.

The Premier, though, was not the only member of government who sought out the TV cameras to refute my interpretation of events and recast me as a troubled woman who wasn't dealing well emotionally with my circumstances.

Ravi Kahlon, the Government House Leader, dismissed the idea that I had experienced antisemitism in the caucus.

"No, I would not agree with that," he told a scrum in the Legislature, including the *Vancouver Sun*'s Katie DeRosa. "We are always speaking out against hate towards any community."

It is not considered best practices in antiracism to deny people's expressed lived experience with discrimination, so perhaps the government thought that the South Asian guy might be the most effective messenger for that soundbite. Ravi also opined that "Selina is clearly hurting," which was a loaded phrase.

Yes, I was hurting. Because I was betrayed by my colleagues and my leader. Rather than take any responsibility for that situation, there was a reference to my emotional state. Given all the possible things he might have said in that moment, referencing a woman colleague's emotions might not have been the most constructive approach.

Next up was George Heyman. He was trotted out to weigh in on my assessment.

"I grew up as a Jew," he told the assembled media.

"My experience," George told media, "is that our caucus and our cabinet is deeply committed to fighting antisemitism, to opposing hatred, and I have found them to be personally supportive of me on an ongoing basis at any time since October, when they have felt that I might be feeling strong emotions about what is going on. They've regularly checked in with me. They've regularly expressed their commitment to fighting antisemitism."

This looked to me like the tokenism that the antisemitic mobs employ, pointing to the rare Jew who agrees with their perspective.

What was most interesting about George emerging at this particular moment was that he had never before, in the 11 years that I had worked with him, stood up and said, "I'm a Jew, let me handle this. Let me be the voice for the Jewish community." He had always left that work for me to do.

After I opened myself up to express my experiences with antisemitism and isolation within cabinet and caucus, suddenly it seemed George had found his voice as a Jew—and then only to contradict my experience.

It is perhaps a symptom of my faith in humanity—or my naïveté—that such statements could continue to surprise me. It was, by that point, precisely what I should have expected.

While I felt utterly alone in the environment of my colleagues, I was surrounded by enveloping support among the people who mattered.

In the days and weeks after I left caucus, the emails and notes that I received continued to buoy me. MLAs from opposition parties were especially kind.

The Jewish community was overwhelmingly supportive. I heard from so many people individually. Many of them were not New Democrats, and in some cases had not been enthusiastic of my efforts to build bridges between the NDP and the Jewish community. But when I was betrayed, they took this personally. Now I was *their* Selina. My treatment at the hands of a government that did not live up to their expressed commitment to anti-racism, multiculturalism, diversity and inclusion was an affront to them.

One of the first Jewish community events I attended after all this happened was Vancouver's commemoration of Yom Hazikaron, Israel's remembrance day for fallen soldiers and victims of terrorism.

This is always a solemn day of mourning, like November 11, but this was the first such commemoration since October 7. The pain was fresh, intense and palpable. Like on Remembrance Day, audiences are subdued and there is no applause. On this night, though, when my presence was acknowledged, the hundreds of attendees rose to their feet and gave me a thunderous ovation.

This almost overwhelmed me—and it was discomforting in some ways, not least because of the seeming breach in decorum it represented. It was discomforting also because I do not feel I did anything to deserve such a response. I had not *done* something so much as I had something done *to me.*

I have had time to ponder the impetus of that ovation. While we were gathered to grieve and to memorialize Jews lost in defence of our homeland, we were also collectively facing a separate conflict closer to home, and I was one of the most visible symbols of that struggle.

Jews were all living in a changed world after October 7. Where we had counted on our elected leaders to empathize with us and to act not only in the interest of Jewish British Columbians but in the interest of our collective multicultural harmony, we had been grievously disappointed.

Probably every person in that room, in the previous months, had been hurt by people they thought were their friends, betrayed by dear ones, subjected to intentional and unintentional harms by those around them. As much as I had, each of them had their own individual experiences with antisemitism, though in perhaps less public ways, and had been told, explicitly or implicitly, that it was all in their heads. They were made to feel that their feelings were invalid, their identities were not deserving of the same respect we provide to others. The clear message they had received from screaming protesters was that our people are not as worthy of life as others. From the leaders who remained silent, the message they received was that the mobs were right. They had learned that they have neighbours who think the brutal deaths of Jews are not worth mourning.

My community's applause was not so much an expression of gratitude for me, but a recognition that we are all experiencing this together. Although each of our experiences has been different, I embodied for them the range of unprecedented anxieties and betrayals that probably every Jew in the room was going through. I represented, in that moment, our collective anguish that a province, a country and a world we thought we knew turned almost on a dime into a place we hardly recognized. In the face of all this disenchantment, we were together. We were not alone. We could depend on one another, even if there were others upon whom we could not depend.

This, of necessity, is an essence of Zionism. It is also a core Jewish value. *Kol Yisrael arevim zeh la'zeh* is a concept that underpins our collective identities as Jews and as Zionists: "All Jews, *Kol Yisrael*, are responsible one for another."

Their applause was a statement of defiance, of determination, that we would stand together, come what may, and not allow any single one of us to be separated from the flock or abandoned to the betrayal of others. We were, in that moment, absolutely unified and unbowed.

That my community saw me as a paradigm of what they were all experiencing was humbling. Their solidarity and kindness uplifted me.

Kindness came to me from so many directions.

Amid all the cruelty and indifference I had experienced, there was so much compassion from so many. Strangers sent words of support. The people of Coquitlam-Maillardville helped to heal my broken heart. From the person walking by me in Mundy Park who made a heart shape with her hands as I passed by her, and the cashier at my local grocery store who thanked me for standing up for what is right, to Mary, who stopped me while shopping, introduced herself and thanked me for my service to our community and acknowledged the contributions I made as an MLA and as a cabinet minister. This is what has been mending my broken heart.

These are the people who know who I am and what I represent. It's not the lies, the haters, the gaslighting and the cowardly, performative politicians that matter in the end. It's the people who clearly recognize injustice when they see it. They can tell, no matter the specifics of an issue at hand, the moral difference between a public official targeted for who she is and her attackers, who are motivated by ideological rigidity, malice and political expediency.

These people can tell right from wrong, even when their leaders cannot.

# *Conclusion: Looking Ahead with Hope*

IN 2016, A GUNMAN murdered 49 people and wounded another 53 in the Pulse nightclub, an Orlando, Florida, gay bar.

Imagine if, a few days after that unprecedented, horrific mass murder, an instructor at a British Columbia college stood at an anti-gay rally outside the Vancouver Art Gallery and called the killing of those gay people an "amazing, brilliant offensive."

While no one called the Pulse nightclub mass murder an "amazing, brilliant offensive," those precise words were spoken on the steps of the Vancouver Art Gallery after the October 7 mass murder of almost 1,200 people in Israel, most of them Jews.

If those words had been expressed about the Pulse attack, there is not a doubt in my mind that the instructor would have been fired on the spot. If she had not been fired, I suspect the students at her college, and plenty more, would have marched, if not rioted, until she was.

But that is not what happened. The hateful comments of a college instructor were just a news item people scanned and moved past. There was no uprising of outrage or disgust. It was just another story about hate toward Jews.

This is one of far too many small and large examples of Jews and antisemitism being treated differently from other groups and their experiences with racism and discrimination.

At a time when Canadians are having imperfect, yet ambitious, societal dialogues about race, gender, sexual identities, reconciliation and other tough subjects, the experiences of Jews and antisemitism seem to be a discussion we steadfastly refuse to have.

We need to talk about it. Then we need to act.

## *Solomon's wisdom*

There are moments when your soul feels like it is being split in two.

In the biblical story of King Solomon, the wise king famously determined the rightful mother of a child by ordering the baby cut in half and shared between the two women claiming it. The mother who abandoned her claim to avoid the bisecting of the child was determined to be the real mother and awarded the baby.

I do not have the wisdom of Solomon. I'm also not sure if I am the mother or the baby in this analogy. But in the midst of the crisis between me and my Premier and caucus, I felt absolutely torn in two. As I have reflected on these feelings, I have concluded that I never surrendered my wholeness.

I will always be the bleeding-heart Jew, the social democrat, the progressive. But the people who I thought shared my values proved, when it mattered most, that they and I are more different than we knew.

This emerged not only around Israel and Palestine. In a way, in the end, it wasn't about that at all.

It was about believing members of a community when they say they are under siege. It was about respecting the lived experience of a person when she says she is experiencing racism. It was about putting aside whatever misgivings, political calculations and prejudices we might carry and standing with a besieged community. It was, simply, about knowing what the right thing is and doing it.

Or, in the case of my former colleagues, *not* doing it.

While my heart was shattered and my faith in the people I had worked with so closely and devotedly was broken, when the dust settled, I realized that my values and my various identities have remained absolutely intact. I will always be a Jew and my commitment to social and economic justice have never changed.

Those whose identities were ruptured in this story are the colleagues who have built lives and careers on the idea they are advocates of equality, fairness, antiracism and inclusion. When push came to shove, they shoved me out—but in the process they severed themselves from the values they thought they embodied.

Despite a world insisting that I cannot be both progressive and Zionist, I know that there is no contradiction in these identities. Indeed, to be a progressive and anything other than a Zionist should evoke cognitive dissonance.

To be a Zionist is to stand with the only democracy in the Middle East, the only place where women, LGBTQ+ people, and religious and ethnic minorities are legally equal. To oppose Zionism, which is nothing other than the belief that Jewish people have the right to national self-determination, is an extremist, illiberal position. To oppose Zionism while supporting the national self-determination of every other people is antisemitic.

While many people took from my experience the lesson that Zionism and progressivism are incompatible, this is the wrong message entirely. On the contrary. The message from my experience is that progressives who oppose (or do not actively defend) Zionism betray Jews and, by extension, their own values of inclusivity and antiracism.

I did experience a conflict, there is no doubt. But that conflict was not between my progressive values and my Jewish/Zionist values. It was between my core identity and *other people's values.*

The people with whom I had conflict were self-described progressives who have a problem with my identity as a Zionist and my identity as a Jew.

They didn't suddenly discover I wasn't who I am. I discovered they weren't the people I thought they were.

If they interrogated their own motivations and deepest recesses, they too might realize that they are not the people they thought they were.

In their defence, I don't think most of my former colleagues are antisemitic. The lesson is not quite so simple.

Antisemitism is complex and manifests in countless ways. It is often more subtle and unconsciously ingrained than some other forms of bias and discrimination. This is a complexity that requires a degree of dedication to understand and unlearn. I think that many have not done this work to discover the myriad forms antisemitism can take and therefore have not equipped themselves with the capacity to recognize and adequately confront it. This is a shortcoming that progressive leaders in government (and everywhere) need to address.

There are lessons from my experience that transcend my personal story. There are lessons for our democracy about the necessity to stand up to coercion from interest groups and harassment from mobs. There are lessons for leaders about how to act (and how not to act) when presented with choices between what is easy but wrong and difficult but right. There are lessons about speaking up rather than remaining silent.

The leadership lesson from all this, for me, boiled down to two remarkably simple principles: The first is knowing the right thing to do. The second is doing it.

Several of my former colleagues were sympathetic. They offered moral support to me as an individual. A few expressed some sympathy for the larger issues facing Jewish British Columbians. I know some share my basic approach to peace between Israelis and Palestinians.

But they were quiet allies. Not one of them was willing to be an ally out loud. A quiet ally is better than an enemy. But their impact on quelling antisemitism is negligible.

I know that some of my former colleagues would have liked to have been publicly supportive but, seeing what happened to me, opted instead to stay silent. I get that.

Even so, we enter public life to make change. Change often demands the courage to make tough decisions. Surely fighting racism—within our own ranks, no less—deserves the courage to expend whatever political capital we might have.

It seemed to me that, by refusing to stand up to the mob, the Premier and our caucus empowered and rewarded them. By caving to the coercion—some have used the term blackmail—of a small cluster of Islamic clergy and organizations, the Premier and the caucus folded when they should have held firm.

Does this make them antisemitic? Hardly.

So where does antisemitism fit in all this?

In antiracist discourse, as I mentioned much earlier, there is a concept that there is no such thing as "nonracist." There is only racist or antiracist. Racism is not a topic where sitting on the fence is a tolerable option.

I have identified a few colleagues who acted out in ways that I perceive as antisemitic. Others didn't give me proof but sent off vibes. I know this sounds vague but I think people of colour and queer people might know what I mean. There's a discomfort, an awkwardness, an elephant in the room, averted eye contact, an abrupt change of subject. It's not proof. It's a gut feeling.

These were a very small group of my colleagues.

What was a slap in the face was the absolute, comprehensive, total silence of every single other member of the NDP caucus. This has been the truly heart-rending realization from all of this.

There have always been some who hate Jews or, for whatever reasons, will betray and harm us. Jews know that.

What has shocked, disappointed and alarmed us is the pervasive silence of the good people. The acts of commission, of overtly hurtful or even antisemitic expressions by the few—Jews are used to that. The acts of omission, the decision by those we thought were our friends to keep quiet in the face of everything that is happening—that is the real injury.

When every member of the progressive, antiracist government of which I was a member chose public silence in the face of injustice, this was a turning point.

It was a turning point for me, obviously. I was fired from cabinet and then alienated, which forced me out of caucus.

It was also a turning point for my former colleagues, for our government and for progressive movements in ways they have not even begun to comprehend.

Of course, we do not have the power to see inside someone's heart to decisively discern their motivations, so I can't prove this or that former colleague is antisemitic or not antisemitic.

I can be 100 percent certain, however, that I can count on one hand the number of my former colleagues who are *anti*-antisemitic.

## Dangers to democracy

There are extremists on a huge range of issues. As long as there are leaders ready to push back against those who use threats, intimidation and blackmail, our democracy remains secure.

But when leaders surrender to these sorts of behaviours, when they yield in the face of threats rather than hold fast to what is right, democracy is endangered.

Even if one does not care about Israel or Palestine, I believe that what the Premier did to me is a dangerous development. The effect a mob of activists and a small group of clergy had in the course of a weekend is a template for small groups of extremists no matter their cause.

Anti-gay, anti-choice and other activists are no doubt analyzing the strategy that got me fired to see if it can be retrofitted for their purposes. Fanatical groups with minority viewpoints, whose opinions will never win converts or elections, learned the lesson that if you can threaten chaos at party fundraisers, make life miserable for elected officials and spread hyperbolic accusations then, depending on the backbone of the person at the top, you just might get what you want.

Faced with a baying mob and, possibly more crucially, pressures from Muslim clerics and Islamic organizations, it appears that David Eby's desire to make the noise stop is his preferred action, no matter the consequences.

It certainly appeared to me that the Premier was acting out of political expediency. Then he went before TV cameras and seemed to cast my firing as an act of antiracist principle.

The principle, in the end, had little or nothing to do with racism or even with Israel and Palestine. It had to do with the role of religion and its representatives in civil society. It had to do with a cultural community extracting political vengeance on a perceived adversary by threatening to withhold from one political party access to their voters. It had to do with allowing a small but loud cluster of activists to disrupt democratic processes. At its absolute core, the principle was simply the tension between doing what is right but difficult or what is wrong but easy.

This is a scary proposition for democracy. I worry that this kind of leadership almost guarantees that next time, no matter who the single-issue zealots are or what they hope to extract from the government, they will know that intimidation, bullying and threats are effective tactics. Because they worked the last time.

There is a variable here. The groups that attacked me were perceived to be on "our side." "Pro-Palestinian" activists are associated with the NDP far more than with the other main party. This may have made it more difficult for the Premier to withstand the pressure. Anti-vaxxers, homophobes, NIMBYs—these are not core constituents of New Democrats. Perhaps people are easier to ignore when they aren't going to vote for you anyway.

That shouldn't matter though. Doing the right thing means doing the right thing no matter what. I believe that if leaders refuse to stand up to intimidation and coercion, whatever the source, they are not deserving of the term leader.

* * *

I faced a dramatically changed circumstance after David Eby fired me. But so did the ones I left behind when I was fired from cabinet and when I quit the New Democrat caucus.

In this context, I was the lucky one.

I was free. My head was held high. My former colleagues learned in no uncertain terms the wisdom of keeping their heads down, of remaining silent.

I know from talking to some of my former colleagues that they learned from my example a stark lesson about the value of not making waves. Go along to get along. Avoid anything that could even possibly provoke controversy. Stay quiet. Don't take a stand.

This undermines the effectiveness of every single elected official and compromises our entire legislative system.

* * *

Throughout history, standing with the Jewish people has been especially difficult when masses of very angry people mobilize against Jews. But let's get some perspective. While Jews in British Columbia are facing racism and isolation, this is not a time when standing with us takes the kind of courage it has demanded at other moments in history.

A lesson I hope readers will take from all this is the cost of being silent and the necessity of speaking up.

One of the reasons more Canadians have not stood with the Jewish community even as opinion surveys indicate they would like to is, I think, because they have not been given tangible, actionable ways to do so. These are what I leave you with.

I hope you will read these, then act.

# *Calls to Action*

IF YOU HAVE READ this far, I hope that means you are committed to standing against antisemitism. I don't expect you to agree with everything I have written. But I hope you accept my basic premise that there is a problem—and I hope that you are willing to be part of the solution.

Constructive actions in the face of tough challenges are the key to tikkun olam. To repair the broken world, to make the world a better place, we need to act—and we need a blueprint for how a better world will look and a work plan for getting there.

I share these ideas from my experience, from my reading, from my engagement with Jews and non-Jews. These are not by any means definitive answers. And let us not kid ourselves that a millennia-old problem will be resolved in a day. However, the journey of many miles begins with a single step.

Rabbi Tarfon, a Talmudic sage, made our responsibilities clear: "It is not your duty to complete the work, but neither are you free to desist from it."

## *What individual Jews can do*

### Refuse to hide

I know Jews who have taken down their mezuzah, the case that Jews put on our doorpost that contains a Hebrew blessing. Others have removed Jewish-identifying jewellery. Some parents have pulled their children out of public school and placed them in Jewish day schools. Other Jewish families even moved neighbourhoods, to where there is a greater presence of Jewish people.

I can appreciate the desire to hide, to be among those who understand. We are less likely to experience the wallop of unexpected verbal or emotional assaults when we are among our own. Many of us have stopped listening to radio, watching TV or engaging on social media because a harmless pastime can quickly send us into an emotional spiral.

But this has long-term consequences. By sequestering ourselves, we make our already small numbers and limited voices even smaller and quieter.

Personal security is always paramount. We must not put ourselves in situations where we risk danger to our person or our family. But this moment does demand courage. There will be emotional hurt. We may have to push our boundaries of comfort. But hiding will not solve the larger problem. It will make it worse.

It is more important now than ever—we have to turn outward.

We need to openly celebrate who we are, take pride in our unique identity. That is a core tenet of what it means to be Canadian—and if Jews cannot do that in Canada, then we, and our country, are truly in trouble.

It would be easier to hide. But if protecting future generations is our obligation, we need to demonstrate courage today.

I believe we can do that—and to make sure we and our country do not descend into deeper trouble, we *must* do it.

### Stand (y)our ground

We have a right to be here. We have a right to have a Jewish life in Canada (and everywhere in the world, including in Israel). We have a right to live our lives in peace and we have a right to push back against hatred.

We need to stand our ground.

This means taking the time to let people know that their words and actions have impacts. It means finding the courage to tell friends, colleagues and strangers that their words are hurtful. It means having the vulnerability to share our perspectives with them.

Standing our ground doesn't mean putting ourselves in harm's way or getting into shouting matches. It does mean finding our voice and using it.

My first foray into politics was standing at a Coquitlam City Council meeting, my voice trembling, my hands shaking the paper I was reading from. A decade-and-a-half later, I was a senior minister in BC's government, taking questions on the Legislative Assembly floor.

Courage is a muscle. Exercise it.

**Stand with Israel**

The inclination to hide our identity is probably never greater than when it comes to our identity as Zionists. It's hard to stand with Israel right now. In a huge number of venues where we should not have to fear for our emotional or physical security, "coming out" as a Zionist puts us at serious risk. In many spaces, it is a sure path to shunning. That's what happened to me.

People who will stand with us against antisemitism will not stand with us against anti-Zionism. People who condemn attacks on us because we are Jews justify attacks on us because we are Zionists.

Like the futility of hiding as a Jew, we cannot hide as Zionists. Yes, be prudent. Don't wave an Israeli flag at an anti-Israel march. We have the legal right to do so, but judiciousness suggests it is unwise.

However, when safe to do so—and each of us must assess what is safe for ourselves—let your figurative or literal Israeli flag fly!

Showing we have the courage of our convictions is an important step in demonstrating that we will not be cowed. It is also a message to potential allies that it is safe and necessary to stand with us.

**Engage respectfully or not at all**

Shouting hateful things isn't going to change minds. Humiliating others isn't going to help them understand how their words, actions and silence are hurtful.

Engaging in a dialogue that seeks understanding is the work we have to do and we have a lot of work to do. This isn't easy work, but it must be done.

We can quickly tell when someone is motivated by goodwill or ill-will. Engage with the former. Walk away from the latter.

**Be the "Jew in the Crew"**

Many Jews are already deeply engaged in all facets of the broader world we live in. We are represented in all professions and we volunteer throughout our own Jewish communities and in the broader community. We have friends of every race, every religion and every opinion.

We need to do more of this. While our reflex right now may be to surround ourselves with people like ourselves, we have an obligation and a privilege, a *mitzvah*, to engage with the wider world.

By turning away from the non-Jewish world, our absence creates a vacuum that allows others to depict us in ways that are not accurate or fully formed.

We need to redouble our efforts to be present in every single space. I know we are all doing a lot of heavy lifting already. But this is important.

We need to volunteer our time to sit on committees, to run for union leadership, to volunteer for non-Jewish charities, to sit on university boards and to join parent advisory committees in public schools. We need to coach sports teams and join community choirs. We need to invite neighbours and friends to join us for our holidays. We need to bring our Jewish voices to all these places so that people know who we are as Jews and as humans.

In other words, we all need to be the Jew in the Crew.

**Don't throw up our hands**

I received a lovely note just after I was fired from cabinet. It was from a young person who went to public elementary school with my daughter, 25 years ago. My two kids made up half the Jewish population of their elementary school. I wanted my children to have a strong Jewish identity, so I made it a mission to expose their teachers and classmates to every Jewish holiday.

This young woman remembered this exposure to our traditions and those small gestures stayed with her all these years. She understood, at least in a small way, who we are.

Public education is the greatest equalizer in our society. It is where we first experience pluralism and develop an understanding of what it means to live in a diverse world. Public schools are where we are exposed to different people, who have different experiences, ideas and beliefs. The anti-Jewish activism that we are seeing in teachers' unions across this country sends the message that Jewish children (and teachers) are unwelcome in public schools. It sends a larger message, though. It is a threat to the cherished lessons of tolerance, inclusivity and diversity that are among the most central lessons kids are supposed to learn. This activism is not only harming Jews. It is rotting the very core of our public education system.

I appreciate the angst that many Jewish parents are feeling and I get that some want to pull their kids from public school. But we need to address the problem at its root. Our absence will actually make antisemitism worse.

Of course, we are small in number. We can't do it alone. We have to reach out to our neighbours and friends and ask for their help. We need to give them specific, tangible ways to be allies. I have a few modest suggestions . . .

## *What individual non-Jews can do*

If there is a single, overriding message I want people to take from this book, it is that Jews need non-Jewish allies.

Quiet allies are nice. They are better than enemies. But sending heart emojis doesn't really do much. We need people to speak up. If you are willing to be an ally, here are some steps to consider . . .

### Use your voice

We need your voices. Jews can't effectively stand up to antisemitism alone. We simply lack the numbers.

Every one of us has a circle of influence: Our friends, our colleagues, our volunteer groups, our book clubs, every affiliation we have.

We are not reinventing the wheel here. We have learned to do this. We have, most of us, learned to push back against misogyny in the workplace, against racism at the family dinner table, against homophobia, anti-Indigenous bigotry, ageism, ableism, sizeism. We know how to do this!

Learn the many forms antisemitism can take and then contest it everywhere it appears in your circles of influence.

Then broaden your circles of influence. Contact businesses, elected officials, boards of directors and business managers when you see something that needs challenging. Send a letter to the editor. Call a phone-in program. Attend a rally or vigil. Be the voice of dissent in your union, your workplace, your classroom, your church. Wherever you are, your voice goes with you. Use it.

We need elected leaders to know that non-Jewish constituents care about these issues. Jews make up one percent of Canada's electorate—and we are concentrated in just a handful of communities and ridings. Allies can have an outsized impact by speaking out on these issues.

**Really defend free expression**

Many people don't seem to realize that free speech goes both ways. Too often, we hear hateful words and let them pass. In some cases, we ignore these words of hate because it is easier to ignore them. At other times, we let them pass because we assume that, in a free country, people have the right to express atrocious ideas. They do. But you have rights too. You have a right to contest those atrocious ideas. Use your free expression to denounce language that incites hatred and violence.

**Engage with Jews**

This is not as easy as it sounds. Today's reality means that unfamiliar faces showing up at a Jewish community event can raise security concerns. But take a moment to reach out to Jewish organizations and let them know you are an ally and see if there is a constructive way to engage.

Visit a Holocaust education centre or attend a commemorative event. There are literally hundreds of lectures sponsored by Jewish organizations across Canada every year on topics that will boggle (and inspire) your mind. Arrange a reciprocal visit between your church, mosque or other congregation and a synagogue. Invite a speaker to your kids' class. Watch Jewish films and read Jewish books. Volunteer with a Jewish organization that appeals to you.

Start with the "Community Directory" of your nearest Jewish Federation. (Just Google "Jewish Federation" and your nearest city.) Even if you don't live near an organized Jewish community, technology allows anyone to virtually attend countless Jewish activities every year.

This engagement will help you understand—and that will make you a better advocate for multiculturalism, inclusion and Canadian values.

## *What we can do as a society*

As a society, we need to act. Antisemitism is a social problem. We also need to confront it collectively. Here are a few suggestions . . .

### Test our laws

I believe that the law is a recourse of last resort. Especially when dealing with racism and other forms of bias, by the time we get the law involved, we have already passed a tipping point. Education, public awareness and dialogue are the antidotes to these problems.

But the law has a place. We have witnessed people and groups explicitly celebrating the mass murders of Jews, and calling for more. We need to test our hate laws—and if the courts say they're not applicable, we need to press Parliament to strengthen the laws.

### Protect our students

A university is supposed to challenge students and be a place of debate and intellectual conflict. But it should be a place of conflict *around ideas*, not conflict against people.

What we have seen in Canada recently is intolerable bullying and targeting of Jewish students. Jews have been alarmed and concerned about the situation on campuses not only because our kids and grandkids are there and we fear for their physical and emotional safety. We are alarmed because, if our campuses are not safe for Jews today, our country may not be safe for Jews tomorrow. Universities and colleges are where Canadian leaders of the future are formed. Jews have reason to worry.

Canadian campuses have been teeming with hateful signage and rhetoric, even vandalism and violence. This is not legitimate expression. And we do not need courts or police to determine this. Universities and colleges have standards of behaviour. They need to enforce them. When they don't, we need students, parents, alumni and donors to make sure they do.

**Nurture real inclusion**

When people don't feel connected to something—a community, a set of values, an identity—they may lack of sense of purpose and seek out something that gives them belonging and meaning. This may be especially true since COVID left so many people, especially the young, feeling isolated and disconnected.

The longing to feel connection is a powerful force. And along came an activist movement that seems to offer meaning and belonging—and a chance to blow off some pent-up steam.

Unfortunately, in many ways, the anti-Israel movement that so many have latched onto is descended from a very old movement, one of humankind's oldest forms of groupthink and othering.

We need to strengthen communities that give young people a sense of purpose and belonging. This is a huge undertaking but we are not starting from nothing. We have existing, strong communities. We need to empower them and ensure they have what young people are looking for. We also need to emphasize in-person interactions and address young people's (and older people's) engagement with electronic screens. But that is the topic of other books.

Where young people lack a sense of belonging and purpose, they become susceptible to radicalization, self-harm and other dangers. We need to support sports teams, arts and cultural activities for young people and other groups that help to create face-to-face interactions.

We need to ensure that our young people learn critical thinking approaches and employ them to properly research and analyze what they are reading and hearing. These are skills they need to process information that comes at them—on every subject—through their social media channels.

**Treat antisemitism the way we treat other forms of racism**

Canadians need to learn how Jewish identity is similar to and different from other racial, religious, national and ethnocultural identities, because there is a lot of confusion around this and confusion can lead to misinformation.

Canadians need to learn these things so that we can recognize when we are treating Jews and antisemitism differently than we treat other people and their experiences.

See the recommended resources at the end of this book.

**Begin the dialogue**

The crisis we now see is a result of our failure as a society to have necessary, hard conversations about Jews and antisemitism.

We have done this before. The Canadian Truth and Reconciliation Commission and other national conversations we have had—guided by Black Lives Matter or the #MeToo movement and other dialogues devoted to equality and acceptance for people of all racial, gender, physical, emotional and other differences—are appropriate models for this conversation.

This can take many forms. I invite you to stay in touch at selinarobinson.ca. I don't know where this dialogue will take us. But I hope you will be a part of it.

# *Final Reflections*

TO COMMUNITY LEADERS and those who aspire-to-be leaders—in government, in your careers, in the social sector, as activists—whatever role you seek to take on in your version of tikkun olam, I share what wisdom I have accumulated so far in my time as a servant to my community.

Here are the final words I spoke in the BC Legislature, on May 13, 2024:

> *Mr Speaker, my parting words in this place are for those who decide to put their name forward for public office—I want to speak to those folks directly:*
>
> *Know yourself and your values.*
>
> *There is no such thing as the perfect political party, just the party of best fit.*
>
> *Yes, you need a thick skin, but make sure that it's not so thick that you no longer feel the pain of others.*
>
> *Come into this business with your integrity and be sure to leave with your integrity.*
>
> *Be courageous.*
>
> *If you get yourself elected, recognize the privilege to serve ALL the people you represent, not just those who supported or voted for you.*

* * *

I can be faulted for many things. But in the face of all the challenges and disappointments, I am confident I stood firm on who I am and what I represent.

This story, however, is about something much larger. It is about antisemitism, the many ways it can take shape and the manner in which even progressive, antiracist leaders can excuse and perpetrate it.

It is about leadership—real, courageous leadership—which can be positively demonstrated through actions, or demonstrated by negative example in its absence.

It is about the hopefulness of endeavouring to repair the broken, unfinished world through ceaseless striving for individual and collective improvement. We will never be perfect. The world will never be faultless. But repairing the world must always be our guiding star. Our reach must always exceed our grasp.

When I reflect on leadership, I retain a certainty that good people and good leaders will prevail.

The optimist in me knows that people almost invariably recognize the difference between right and wrong. I know that there are many people who want to better understand complex issues and conflicts, who are not satisfied to share simplistic memes on social media. I know that most people value our democracy and the healthy exchange of ideas.

In the end, I believe that devotion to what is good and hopeful and possible is greater than hatred, blame and derision. I know that there are more people ready to fight for what is fair and just than there are those prepared to give up.

I will be an optimist to the very end. I have always subscribed to the Jewish adage that it is better to light a candle than to curse the darkness.

Has anyone ever encapsulated these hopes better than Jack Layton did in his final words to us?

"My friends, love is better than anger. Hope is better than fear. Optimism is better than despair. So let us be loving, hopeful and optimistic. And we'll change the world."

---

# *Acknowledgements*

WRITING THIS BOOK would not have happened without the encouragement and support of many.

Thank you to Pat Johnson who first suggested that I write this book and then helped me weave my experiences and ideas into a manuscript.

Thank you to all those who read earlier versions of the manuscript as we shaped it into its current form: Marilyn Craig, Ivan Crothers, Vera Frinton, Sandra Hochstein, Vicki Huntington, Terry O'Neill, Cynthia Ramsay, Dan Robinson and Don Wright.

Thank you to those who helped to finance this project—you know who you are.

I want to take a moment to thank the public service who helped me to be a good minister of the Crown, ensuring that I always had options to consider before making any decision on behalf of British Columbians. Kaye Krishna, Heather Wood and Bobbi Plecas, along with their teams, all served me as excellent Deputy Ministers putting the needs of British Columbians at the forefront of their commitment to public service.

I have to thank the people who love me most in the world, for being my guiding light and the reason I use my voice: my dad Irv Dardick, my mom Rhoda Dardick (of blessed memory), my in-laws, Sandra and Gary Robinson, and my children and their spouses, Aaron and Kyle Demes and Leya Robinson and Omer Gigi.

Running for elected office and serving British Columbians would not have been possible without the love, support and encouragement of my best friend and husband Dan Robinson, who first committed to support me in whatever I wanted to do back in 1985 and has never backed away from that commitment—I am lucky to have him in my life.

Thank you to the voters of Coquitlam-Maillardville, who put their trust in me to represent them in Victoria.

Finally, I want to thank all of those people who reached out with kind words after I was fired from cabinet. I am deeply indebted to you as each note, each letter, each email helped put my broken heart back together piece by piece.

With love,<br>
S

# *Resources for Further Exploration*

A small, subjective sampling of resources for those who want to know more.

## *Online Resources*

### Jewish & Israeli Culture, History & People

Centre for Jewish History
cjh.org

Jewish Virtual Library
jewishvirtuallibrary.org

My Jewish Learning
myjewishlearning.com

### Antisemitism

Canadian Handbook on the IHRA Working Definition of Antisemitism
canada.ca/en/canadian-heritage/services/canada-holocaust/antisemitism/handbook-definition-antisemitism.html

Facing History & Ourselves
facinghistory.org

Institute for the Study of Global Antisemitism and Policy
isgap.org

Upstanders Canada
upstanderscanada.com

World Jewish Congress
worldjewishcongress.org/en

### Holocaust

Anne Frank House
annefrank.org

Auschwitz-Birkenau Memorial and Museum
auschwitz.org

Vancouver Holocaust Education Centre
vhec.org

Yad Vashem—The World Holocaust Remembrance Center
yadvashem.org

## *Books*

### Jewish Culture, History & People

*Book of Jewish Values (The)*, by Joseph Telushkin

*Canada's Jews: A People's Journey*, by Gerald J. J. Tulchinsky

*To Heal a Fractured World*, by Jonathan Sacks

### Israeli Culture, History & People

*Can We Talk About Israel?: A Guide for the Curious, Confused, and Conflicted*, by Daniel Sokatch

*Israel: A Concise History of a Nation Reborn*, by Daniel Gordis

*Israel: A Simple Guide to the Most Misunderstood Country on Earth*, by Noa Tishby

*Letters to My Palestinian Neighbor*, by Yossi Klein Halevi

**Antisemitism**

*A Lethal Obsession: Anti-Semitism from Antiquity to the Global Jihad*, by Robert S. Wistrich

*Anti-Judaism: The Western Tradition*, by David Nirenberg

*How to Fight Antisemitism*, by Bari Weiss

*None Is Too Many: Canada and the Jews of Europe 1933–1948*, by Irving Abella and Harold Troper

*People Love Dead Jews*, by Dara Horn

**Holocaust—History**

*Destruction of the European Jews (The)*, by Raul Hilberg

*Holocaust (The): The Jewish Tragedy*, by Martin Gilbert

*War Against the Jews (The)*, by Lucy S. Dawidowicz

**Holocaust—Personal Narratives**

*Maus*, by Art Spiegelman

*Night*, by Elie Wiesel

*Survival in Auschwitz*, by Primo Levi

# *Charitable Recipients*

ALL PROCEEDS from sales of *Truth Be Told* support the following charities.

**The Parents Circle—Families Forum** is a joint Israeli-Palestinian organization of over 700 families, all of whom have lost an immediate family member to the ongoing conflict. The Parents Circle–Families Forum was created in 1995 by a few Israeli families. The first meeting between bereaved Palestinians from Gaza and Israeli families took place in 1998.

These families identified with a call to prevent bereavement, to promote dialogue, tolerance, reconciliation and peace.

The PCFF is registered as a nonprofit organization, professionally managed by a joint Israeli-Palestinian board and a professional team operating from a Palestinian office in Beit Jala and an Israeli office in Ramat Ef'al.

**theparentscircle.org/en**

* * *

**Upstanders Canada** is a grassroots movement to encourage Canadians (especially non-Jewish Canadians) to stand against antisemitism and anti-Zionism.

Upstanders Canada believes Jewish people have the right to live in peace and free from fear everywhere in the world, including in Canada and in Israel.

Upstanders Canada is a registered charity that employs innovative, entrepreneurial, grassroots strategies to encourage intercultural exchange and understanding.

**upstanderscanada.com**

# *About the Cover Art: Torn Fragments of Life*

## *Artist's Statement*

**Kathleen Tennant**

TORN FRAGMENTS of Life was created on the day six hostages, who had survived for almost 11 months in the most unimaginable of circumstances, were found dead. I didn't know what to do with the thoughts that were swirling around in my head. They had survived so long. Their family's pain. Their pain. Their horror. So I ripped up my art and created this piece. Each piece of torn paper placed firmly in place. My thoughts kept going back to Hersh Goldberg-Polin, whose arm had been blown off, and his parents, who did everything possible a parent could do to save their child.

One year ago, my eyes were opened wide to the horror of watching terrorists attack innocent people in the most barbaric and horrific ways possible. Then, I was shocked by the silence of so many, especially in the arts community. How so many people who stood with other minority groups turned their backs on the Jewish community or remained silent. They were not silent on other issues like BLM, LGBTQ+, #MeToo. And yet, when Jewish people were attacked and murdered, there were those who were saying it was justified. I was astonished by how news organizations, schools, educators distorted the truth. I saw the terrorists' propaganda machine working and truth being silenced by the masses. The chanting in the streets, the definition of antisemitism being challenged by those who aren't Jewish, the revisionist history of the Holocaust or the blatant denial that it happened.

People openly carrying the flags of terrorist organizations in Canadian streets.

Torn fragments of life are the voice memos, text messages, phone calls, DMs I received from my Jewish friends and followers thanking me for standing with them. Thanking me for not being silent. I didn't understand why I was being thanked because I was just being me. Peace comes when terrorism is recognized for the evil it is and when that evil is destroyed. I have and always will be against hate. I have and always will stand with humanity. And that will always include those who are Jewish.

Art by Kathleen Tennant
**www.kathleentennant.com**

# *About the Author*

SELINA ROBINSON was born in Montréal and moved to the Vancouver area with her family as a teenager. She holds a master's degree in counselling psychology from Simon Fraser University and has been a family counsellor for most of her career.

She and her husband, Dan, have two adult children and live in Coquitlam, British Columbia.

Robinson held senior positions in a range of social service agencies before entering public life, in 2008, when she became a City Councillor in Coquitlam. She was re-elected in the following election, topping the polls.

In 2013, Robinson was elected as the New Democratic Party Member of the British Columbia Legislative Assembly for Coquitlam-Maillardville. After serving as an opposition critic, she was appointed to cabinet as Minister of Municipal Affairs and Housing when the NDP formed government in 2017.

After the 2020 election, Premier John Horgan appointed Robinson Minister of Finance, where she helped guide the province's economy through the COVID pandemic, resulting in successive surplus budgets.

In 2022, the new Premier David Eby appointed Robinson Minister of Post-Secondary Education and Future Skills.

Robinson, who dubbed herself the "Jew in the Crew," was one of the most prominent Jewish elected officials in Canada. After the terrorist attacks of October 7, 2023, and skyrocketing antisemitism worldwide, Robinson found herself targeted by anti-Israel activists.

After a webinar in early 2024, in which Robinson referred to the territory on which Israel was founded as "a crappy piece of land," she became the centre of a political firestorm, in which activists and a group of Muslim clergy demanded her resignation. She was subjected to online harassment, including a credible death threat, and her constituency office was vandalized with antisemitic graffiti.

Less than a week after making those remarks, Robinson was fired from BC's cabinet by Eby, who said she could not continue with her responsibilities due to the "depth of work" she had to do to repair the harm caused by her comments.

This book is that deep work.

**selinarobinson.ca**